A Borderlands View on Latinos, Latin Americans, and Decolonization

A Borderlands View on Latinos, Latin Americans, and Decolonization

Rethinking Mental Health

Pilar Hernández-Wolfe, PhD, LMFT

JASON ARONSON
Lanham • Boulder • New York • Toronto • Plymouth, UK

Published by Jason Aronson
A wholly owned subsidiary of The Rowman & Littlefield Publishing Group, Inc.
4501 Forbes Boulevard, Suite 200, Lanham, Maryland 20706
www.rowman.com

10 Thornbury Road, Plymouth PL6 7PP, United Kingdom

Copyright © 2013 by Jason Aronson

British Library Cataloguing in Publication Information Available

Library of Congress Cataloging-in-Publication Data
Hernández-Wolfe, Pilar, 1967-
A borderlands view on Latinos, Latin Americans, and decolonization : rethinking mental health / Pilar Hern?ndez-Wolfe.
p. cm.
Includes bibliographical references and index.
ISBN 978-0-7657-0931-8 (cloth : alkaline paper) -- ISBN 978-0-7657-0932-5 (electronic)
1. Mestizos--Mental health--United States. 2. Hispanic Americans--Mental health. 3. Latin Americans--Mental health--United States. 4. Immigrants--Mental health--United States. 5. Decolonization--United States--Psychological aspects. 6. Borderlands--United States--Psychological aspects. 7. United States--Ethnic relations--Psychological aspects. 8. Psychotherapy--United States. 9. Social justice--United States. I. Title.
E184.M47H37 2013
305.868'073--dc23
2012047019
ISBN 978-4422-4775-8 (pbk : alk. paper)

♾™ The paper used in this publication meets the minimum requirements of American National Standard for Information Sciences Permanence of Paper for Printed Library Materials, ANSI/NISO Z39.48-1992.

Printed in the United States of America

Contents

Acknowledgments

I am very grateful to the elders and taitas (shamans) who helped me heal and reconnect with the land of Colombia and my ancestors. This reconnection inspired me and gave me the strength to persist in this work, even in times of doubt or seeming lack of support.

I express my love and gratitude to my friends and colleagues, Jane Ariel, Rhea Almeida, Michael Seltzer, and Nocona Pewewardi, who generously offered their time to review the proposal or earlier drafts of this book. Thanks to Charles Waldegrave for reviewing chapter 5.

Thanks to Mary Beth Hinton for her encouragement, commitment, and technical support, and to the Lewis & Clark College Graduate School of Education faculty research award program, which allowed my work to keep moving at just the right time.

Finally, I am very grateful to Mike, my partner and husband, for his strong and continuing support and for sacrificing so much family time, and to our three four-legged babies, Mindy, Obi, and Max, who have taught me much about love, trauma, recovery, and life, and whose loving beagle barks make our lives fun and connected to all beings.

Preface

I sit in front of my laptop, wondering how to explain the intellectual and emotional meaning that the ideas I present here have for me. I breathe and get grounded. I look through the window and appreciate the day's brightness and the blossoming plants. A feeling of gratitude for life overcomes me. How do I introduce the idea that we can construct therapeutic approaches situated in the borderlands, the in-between spaces? I write from the vantage point of the borderlands.

I was born and raised in Bogotá, a city 2,625 meters above sea level in the mountains of the Andes. I used to see the green and majestic Andes all around Bogotá before the city's population expanded uncontrollably, leading to deforestation and development. The area is nurtured by rivers and lagoons, the Guatavita Lagoon being one of the most magical places. When I was a child, my family and I often traveled around Colombia, especially around the lands where my Muisca ancestors lived, in the highlands and mild-climate flanks comprising today's states of Boyacá, Cundinamarca, and a small part of Santander. I love these lands.

Like most people who live in this region, my skin is brown, my hair is black, and my eyes are brown. We can't trace our ancestry because we became the product of the violence that Spaniards perpetrated on Muisca women. We know we are mixed and we usually call ourselves Mestizos. After many concerted efforts by the Spaniards, the Criollo-led Colombian government, and the Catholic Church—compounded by our peoples' own internalized racism—we almost lost our language, our identity, and our memory. Currently, there is a revival and blossoming of our memory and traditions, and the younger generations are a guiding force; they are also our hope.

I live in Portland, Oregon, now. I am surrounded by the beauty of its trees, rivers, vegetation, and nearby mountains. I also love these lands. I have lived in the United States for almost half of my life. I am fully bilingual and move across some cultures with ease. While in Colombia and some other places in Latin America, I am a part of the ethnic majority, and this gives me many social privileges; in the United States, my ethnic background marginalizes me. The concept of Whiteness varies depending on what society you are in. Many of my Colombian friends and colleagues are shocked when people in the United States tell them that they are not White and that they are a minority. No matter how White they look and how much their last names represent Spanish and other European legacies, they are still perceived as members of an ethnic minority.

The social constructions of privilege and marginalization are complex and not yet complete, but they have material effects on people's lives. I recognize that my gender identity, class, sexual orientation, abilities, nation of origin, and religious background afford me a certain fluidity, depending on specific local contexts (e.g., interacting with others in an academic environment versus shopping in a mall or applying for a car loan). For me, as a brown-skinned Latina, ethnicity is a salient issue in my personal and professional life in the United States. Other dimensions are less salient for me—usually those that place me in locations of privilege, including ability, sexual orientation, religious background, and being middle-class.

I inhabit the borderlands, I worked with displaced populations in Colombia and shared their experiences. I am closely connected to that world on a personal, social, and professional level, because of the political persecution that my own family experienced in generations past, and because of my work, which concerns trauma, resilience, and human rights. I experience a connection with my Indigenous ancestors through a way of thinking that places me as a part of a living world, where the use of plants and the flow of the word have a spiritual dimension and are intertwined with the process of being and learning.

In the borderlands there are translations back and forth; there are clarifications, interpretations, and explanations. There are multiple perspectives and positions on the larger historical processes of colonialism, coloniality, and decolonization. My writing and speaking about these perspectives with those who want to stay in dialogue is an act of resistance; I seek to question epistemic boundaries and to bring the hidden indigenous legacy into the worlds dominated by those who prefer to forget.

I also comfortably travel back and forth among "professional fields" within mental health in the United States. As a graduate of an American Psychological Association (APA)-approved counseling psychology program, I enjoy the benefits of being part of the largest organization of mental health professionals in the United States. I am a family therapist by training and

licensure. I admire the numerous contributions of systemic and deconstruc-
tionist thinkers in family therapy. These epistemologies and the therapeutic
models that developed from them have always seemed naturally akin to how
I think and feel. Thus, most of my work has been produced in the context of
this professional home. I am also a licensed mental health counselor and I led
the Maryland Association for Counseling and Development (MACD) during
2009 through 2010.

I believe that clinical social workers, family therapists, psychologists, and
mental health counselors have fields of knowledge and scopes of practice
that greatly overlap. Although there are distinct specialties and niches in
each, how the professions are defined, their ethical codes, and the therapy
models they practice have more in common than not. However, they compete
with each other and continually stress artificial differences between "professions" and impose hierarchies that supposedly make some superior to others.

In my opinion, these battles are partly tied to the disciplinary compart-
mentalization of Western science, which, in practice, makes distinctions between the fields seem blurry and artificial. The battles are also tied to the
politics of who produces knowledge, how, and for whom, and, of course, to
the capitalist and consumer market economy in which health is a commodity
that some can afford but not others. Thus, professional organizations aggres-
sively compete to break into monopolies of care. In the end, unfortunately,
the business of health, as manifested by managed care, has taken away everyone's capacity to creatively practice and make key decisions about clients'
mental health. Therefore, the cadre of insufficiently educated bureaucrats
that managed care has institutionalized has also taken away fair and deserved
compensation for mental health professionals.

The picture in Colombia is not so different from that in the United States.
The Criollo-led government and the economic elite persist in incorporating
U.S. models of mental health and managed care, especially because those
who have large investments in managed care companies are or were connected with the government through their families. It seems to me that the
time has come for new generations to stand up against the current state of
affairs. Why not? Roy (2004) insisted that there is no discussion in the world
today that is more crucial than that about strategies of resistance. Steve de
Shazer's (1985) miracle question is so pertinent in spaces beyond therapeutic
offices: Suppose that one night while you were asleep there was a miracle,
and private insurance companies were no longer running the mental health
field. How would you know? What would be different?

This book reviews and draws on family therapy and family systems literature as far as therapy is concerned. Besides my personal preference, there are
other reasons for this choice. From its inception, the family therapy movement emerged as a radically different way to address the tasks of healing in
the mental health field. Models from various systemic perspectives offered

their unique conceptual and technical contributions to this task. Structural, strategic, and family-of-origin approaches offered a critique and an alternative to the traditional individual liberal humanism and behaviorism that dominated other mental health fields.

Historically, as the field of family therapy gained status and recognition—as it became official—it adhered progressively to the standards of positivism and neopositivism (a movement in early 20th-century American sociology that blended the three themes of quantification, behaviorism, and positivist epistemology). Then models were put to the tests and trials of objectivity, neutrality, generalization through manualization, and quantification. Subject to the ideals of science, both quantitative and qualitative research have been used to collect, classify, and represent "the other."

Since the 1990s, family therapy approaches emphasizing power, history, and context have been more fully articulated. The feminist contributions to the critique of family therapy models helped advanced the field tremendously by putting issues of power and gender at the forefront of the discussion. Although some of these models address the impact of social realities connected to gender, race, class, and sexual orientation, few address the systematic ways in which the intersectionality of these factors shapes family and community.

In different but not unrelated ways, adherents of both postmodern and decolonization approaches have studied family processes by decentering ethnocentric (Western, heterosexual, White) conceptions of family life. For example, the social-constructionist feminist perspective that has evolved since the 1990s (Avis, 1991; Avis & Turner, 1996; Gosling & Zangari, 1996; Hare-Mustin, 1994; Kliman, 1994; Laird, 1989; McGoldrick, Anderson, & Walsh, 1991; Mirkin, 1994; Weingarten, 1991, 1995) has examined the construction of gender discourses and their implications in day-to-day social practices. Narrative approaches have influenced the field and contributed to the critique of liberal humanistic, cognitive-behavioral, and structural approaches. They provided other ways of looking at therapy that involve deconstructing, reconstructing, and transforming dominant and oppressive discourses and practices.

There are yet other therapy approaches that have gained popularity among scholars and practitioners, and they provide us with a refreshing view of how to think about and undertake the task of healing. I am referring to social justice approaches such as the Just Therapy, feminist, psychology of liberation, and decolonization approaches. These approaches acknowledge that all research is moral and political, and affirm that all inquiry should be ethical, performative, healing, transformative, and participatory. Decolonization approaches would add that inquiry should explicitly address decolonization.

Decolonizing family therapy research engages with individuals, families, and communities' hopes, needs, and goals, and with promises of self-determination, cultural autonomy, and democracy. For example, Duran (2006), Duran and Duran (1995), and Yellowbird (2001) exemplified this type of analysis in their work with First Nations peoples. They offered therapeutic practices based on the belief that acknowledging the Native American genocide, its intergenerational impact, and the appropriateness of reparations will lead to liberating experiences. Specifically, they connected a client family's experience of domestic violence and substance abuse to their peoples' history of violent colonization.

Native American history includes the community's exile onto reservations and the mass kidnapping of their children into Christian boarding homes, where inhumane offenses were perpetrated. The ongoing court battles for the return of stolen lands are evidence of the continued domination of First Nations people. Generating awareness of this history locates the family's troubles within a collective social and political legacy and helps family members recognize that their intrafamilial struggle for wellness and stability is part of a larger communal struggle to regain wholeness and security in the face of the centuries-old colonial holocaust. Within this context, domestic violence and substance abuse are understood not primarily as evidence of family or individual pathology, but as the result of the longstanding institutionalized oppression suffered by a colonized people. The decolonizing family therapists acknowledge that healing is unlikely to come through submission to the expertise of Eurocentric practitioners, for that is the problem masquerading as the solution. Rather, healing will develop through resistance to colonialism.

Latino populations in the United States differ in many ways, including length of time in the country, migration background, ethnicity, geographical location, socioeconomic status, and so on. Some are colonized minorities such as Chicanos and Puerto Riqueños, others came as war and political refugees, others migrated by choice, and others are undocumented migrant workers. The cultural landscapes in the United States and in many Latin American countries are no so different. Issues of diversity, migration, and a history of colonization and *mestizaje* are part of what we live and breathe today in countries like Colombia, Brazil, Perú, México, Chile, Panama, Venezuela, Ecuador, and Argentina.

Given the diversity present throughout South, Central, and North America and the complexity of relationships between South, Central, and North America, the work of "Latin@ psychology," and "Latin@ family therapy" today must offer alternatives to the knowledge produced by "normal science" and assist new generations of Latin@s,[1] Latin Americans, and those involved in Latino culture and Latin America in understanding how the colonization of the Americas is still tied to current issues of migration from the South to the North and within the South, and how mental health practices have emerged from the wound of coloniality.

In this book, the reader will find perspectives of those of us who live in the borderlands—that is, those of us whom Gloria Anzaldúa identified as Mestiz@s, who inhabit the *intersticios*, the spaces in between souls, minds, identities, and geographies. I consider the interplay of colonization, power, privilege, and marginalization in therapy, and I critique Western ideas about the benefits of the pursuit of knowledge. This book offers an alternative foundation for understanding and approaching trauma, identity, and resistance/resilience in working with Latin@s and Latin Americans. Its theory is grounded in the framework of decolonization developed by the modernity/coloniality collective project (Escobar, 2007) and in the pioneering and not-fairly-recognized contributions of Transformative Family Therapy (Almeida, Dolan-Del Vecchio, & Parker, 2007), and Just Therapy (Waldegrave, Tamasese, Tuhaka, & Campbell, 2003).

This paradigmatic shift is situated within the dynamics of coloniality (Mignolo, 2005) and addresses healing as it relates to historical trauma, resistance, resilience, and identities that have been constructed in the borderlands (Anzaldúa, 1987). The decolonization framework for theory and practice building decenters the status quo of inequities that favors the cultural, social, and economic capital of dominant perpetuated by mainstream scholarship in the fields of family therapy, psychology, and counseling.

In sum, this book is a work of connection and integration. I integrate key aspects of the Latin American paradigm proposed by the modernity/coloniality collective project, third-world feminism, Anzaldúa's borderlands theory, and liberation-based family therapy approaches. I integrate the conceptual underpinnings of these bodies of knowledge with very real historical and day-to-day human experiences of trauma, resilience, and resistance.

The spirit of this book is to lovingly affirm the experiences, views, and practices of borderlands, and to invite readers to look through borderland eyes and dare to imagine ways of healing that are contextual, socially and epistemologically equitable, and diverse.

Here is an overview of the book. Chapter 1, Borderland Experiences: Migrations and Crosslinks, discusses the interweaving of borderland experiences, historical trauma, and resilience through case studies in different geographical contexts.

Chapter 2, A New Musical Score, a Horizon, and Possibilities for Meaning Making: A Decolonization Paradigm, examines the underpinnings of the modernity/coloniality collective project. This project utilizes a paradigm, rooted in Latin American thinking, that runs counter to modernist narratives such as Christianity, liberalism, and Marxism, and locates itself at the borders of these systems of thought. It reaches toward ways of thinking that are in contradistinction to Eurocentric philosophies (Escobar, 2007). The modernity/coloniality collective project has been nurtured by liberation theology and philosophy, critical theories of modernity and postmodernity, Chicana feminist theory, South Asian subaltern studies, and African philosophy, among others.

Chapter 3, Nepantla: A Borderland Epistemology, discusses Gloria Anzaldúa's borderland theory in relation to identity, trauma, and resistance/ resilience. I explain an intersectionality framework, discuss relevant contributions from feminist scholars, and highlight the usefulness of these ideas to navigate the borderlands and to address historical trauma. I use case studies from real life to illustrate borderland experiences and intersectionality both in the United States and in Latin American countries.

Chapter 4, Trauma, Resistance/Resilience, and the Colonial Difference, examines three interrelated subjects: traumatic stress, resistance/resilience, and intersectionality. I integrate these subjects using case studies to vividly embody the basics of neurobiology, psychology, and social systems in the lives of people.

Chapter 5, Just and Loving Relationships Heal, discusses the contributions of Transformative Family Therapy (Almeida Dolan-Del Vecchio and Parker, 2007) and Just Therapy (Waldegrave, Tamasese, Tuhaka, and Campbell, 2003). These therapy approaches stand counter to traditional humanistic and individualistic counseling and psychology, to family therapy approaches that lack a connection with issues of power and social context, and to modern and postmodern family therapy approaches that do not integrate equity issues into therapy.

Finally, Chapter 6 invites the reader to consider possible paths for a continued journey in the borderlands.

NOTE

1. Spanish is a gendered language. In some parts of Latin America, writers use the "@" symbol to denote all genders as it would be too onerous to constantly write the feminine, masculine, and gender variant forms for all subjects.

Chapter One

Borderland Experiences

Migrations and Crosslinks

Many communities, families, and individuals are *in between* spiritual, social, political, psychological, and physical spaces. They participate in the making and shaping of relationships in various languages, from and within multiple spaces of marginalization and relative privilege. They inhabit the interstices, or small openings, between dominant worldviews and practices about salvation and progress. In this chapter, I illustrate the interweaving of borderland experiences, historical trauma, and resistance/resilience in different geographical contexts through the stories of Andres and Tatiana and their families and communities. I want to bring to life the complexities, uncertainties, and contradictions that mental health professionals and others who work directly with people may experience, and that are never neat and conceptually organized and linear.

SURVIVAL AND RESISTANCE/RESILIENCE [1]

Andres Martinez was born into a proud family in a central neighborhood in Los Angeles, California, called Pico Union. The Martinez family was one of many Salvadorian families who arrived in the Pico Union neighborhood in the late 1980s as they sought refuge from bloody civil wars that were to last well into the 1990s. When the Martinez family arrived in the neighborhood, they found that many aspects of south-central Los Angeles were not much different than home.

The race riots of the 1960s had left the city in turbulence. Traditionally marginalized African American and Latino communities organized them-

1

selves into protective syndicates that could defend members of their communities in ways that the police force would not. Over time, these protective, locally-based organizations gained more and more power and took on a life of their own. They began to terrorize the neighborhoods and collect protection money from the communities they once served; they acquired many characteristics of other organized crime syndicates that have prevailed in other parts of the United States.

By the time the Martinez family arrived in Pico Union, organized crime syndicates, both Latino and African American, had been waging their own wars for control over territory for black market trade in the city for a decade. Members of these organizations would come to the Pico Union neighborhood and terrorize the small Salvadorian businesses for extortion, sometimes even mistaking them for rival Latino gang members and killing innocent residents.

Eventually, community members had enough. They had left El Salvador to escape the violence from their own governments, paramilitary squads backed by the United States, and insurgents. It was time to organize and fight back the only way they thought they could, and community members decided to align themselves with their own organization. Out of this context an organization called Mara Salvatrucha (MS), later MS-13, was born.

Like a handful of their neighbors, the Martinez Family had been affiliated with MS from the beginning. By the time Andres was born, his father, an exparamilitary soldier of the civil wars, had redevoted himself to the ways of the warrior to protect his family and community. Outside the home, Andres's father, "Tigre," was well known for eliminating "chavalos" (rival gang members). Inside the home, Andres witnessed his father's occasional violence towards his mother and brothers. As the youngest of four sons, Andres managed to steer clear of Tigre's big fists until he was ten. But sometimes, after his brothers received a good beating, their fists would find an easy target in Andres. In his world, the strange mix of threats, fighting, and brotherhood were a part of everyday life.

On his eighth birthday, Andres came home to find his father at the kitchen table with a brand-new Dodgers ball cap and his mother cooking up his favorite dish: fresh chile rellenos. In contrast, on his tenth birthday, he was not greeted by the smell of broiling poblano peppers, but by the hum of their old TV set and his mother's muffled whimpering coming from his parents' bedroom. Concerned for his mother, he stepped through the door. His father looked up from the TV set at Andres, placing a half-empty 40 ounce bottle of malt liquor he had been nursing on the bedside table.

As soon as he met his father's eyes, Andres froze. His father asked with a chuckle, "What, boy, where you expecting a Dodgers uniform today? Birthday gifts and smiles are for little boys. Today, I will give you a true gift for a man!" and slapped him across the face with such great force that Andres fell to the ground. As Andres sat on the floor, his ears rang and he felt a stream of blood trickle out of his nose and over his lips; he opened his eyes to a view of the floor under the stove and a fresh poblano pepper.

After a couple of weeks of abuse at the hands of his father and brothers alike, Andres's mother pulled him aside. Andres thought that finally his mother would protect him. As she gave him money for a soda on his way to school, she looked at him nervously and said, "Andres, you are a good boy. If you stay in school, you can leave this neighborhood and your father would not be able to reach you."

He realized that he had to find a way to protect himself. Later, Andres put a roll of nickels in his palm and ran out to confront his brother Josué, who treated him very poorly. He found Josué on the street outside a nearby apartment complex with other teens. They had been playing baseball when someone knocked the ball into a storm drain. As Josué knelt down to fish out the ball, Andres crept up on his brother quietly. Andres stood right behind his brother, gripped his roll of nickels tightly, called out Josué's name, and punched him square in the nose as he turned around. After several blows, Andres stopped and muttered, "This is your last and only warning. If you ever touch me again, I will catch you and kill you." This was the last time he had to contend with his brother's violence.

At age twelve, Andres approached Sleepy, an ice-cream street vendor, and asked him if he had any work for him to do. Sleepy smiled and invited him into the back of his ice-cream truck. Sleepy gave him twenty, five-dollar bags of crack cocaine to sell. Andres could take half of the earnings. However, a series of events resulted in his removal from the family home. He was later caught selling drugs by the local police, his father was deported, and one of his brothers was sent to a juvenile facility.

When Andres was fourteen, he was taken into his fourth foster home in two years. The middle-age Latino couple with grown children who took him in was very religious and insisted that he go to a Christian religious service with them every Sunday. In this community, he met other teens and men who slowly helped him trust again. The next two years were not free of challenge, but this family and community environment helped him to contain his pain, and to have coherence and stability in his life. He attended counseling on and off and found it helpful at times. He visited with his mother but never went back to her home.

Through the church community, he met Paula, who had a dog and a dog-grooming business. She hired him to look after her dog, Max, while she was away. Max had been rescued from an abusive home and at times was anxious and afraid. Andres realized that he had a seemingly natural ability to connect with Max. His ability to stay calm eased Max's anxiety. Likewise, Max's responsiveness to Andres helped him feel connected, needed, and loved.

Andres began working for her on the weekends. As business grew, many new customers came specifically to seek out the services of Andres. When his foster family allowed him to have his own dog, he went to the local humane society. Once inside, he looked around at all the pens and began to feel frazzled because of all the anxiety and frustration coming from the animals. He could handle several dogs at a time, but this experience was overwhelming.

Andres asked a volunteer at the shelter for help, and the volunteer took him to her personal favorite, a little, stocky black dog named Luna. As Andres let the dog lick his fingers through the chain link, the volunteer talked to him about the common prejudice against black dogs; they were the last to be adopted from shelters, if they were even saved at all. He thought about his own life as a young man of Color and took her home. Luna became his companion and most trusted support when he had bouts of sadness and despair.

Andres attended community college and, in time, became financially independent. He took care of his mother and eventually visited El Salvador with her. In preparing for his trip, he had to face his own feelings of ambiguity about the United States and his idea of El Salvador. He understood spoken Spanish, but did not know how to write or speak and had experienced prejudice for not being "Latino enough." Though he was born in the Unites States, he never felt he truly belonged.

Yet he felt thankful for the people who gave him a hand even when he did not take it. He loved his work with the dogs and his ability to have a meaningful life in the States. He had a girlfriend and a future to look forward to. He always kept his ties with his foster family, their neighborhood, and the Latino Christian church where he found so much support although he did not fully embrace its beliefs. He also learned to live and cope with frequent experiences of blatant racial discrimination and microaggressions.

But most painful of all was learning about the civil war, the U.S. involvement, the El Mozote massacre, the mass exodus abroad, and the ongoing deportation of gang members. As he read in the *San Diego Union Tribune*, gangs were rare in Central America decades ago. After the United States stepped up deportations, gangs became one of Central America's biggest problems. Thousands of violent young men experienced in handling sophisticated weapons and evading law enforcement had been sent back to countries they hadn't seen since they were children. Many barely spoke Spanish. "We've done a great job of exporting the gang culture all over the world," said Al Valdez, supervising investigator of the Orange County District Attorney's Office gang unit. "Now the gang phenomenon is international" (Walker, 2005).

THE RIGHT TO *BE* AND THE JOURNEY TO COEXIST

Tatiana, a Chilean who lived in Santiago, was raised by her mother, Rosario, in a modest home surrounded by a large extended family and in a neighborhood where everyone knew each other's families, and children grew up together playing in the street, a nearby park, and each other's homes. She had never met her father, who left Rosario before Tatiana was born.

Rosario met Ricardo, five years her senior, while she was still an adolescent. Against her parents' wishes she dated him and became pregnant. He too had been born in Santiago. However, his family migrated from the Peruvian highlands, escaping a depressing economic landscape. Like Rosario, Ricardo had olive skin, but his ancestral Indigenous roots were still reflected in the shape of his eyes and face. Though her family did not approve of him, they encouraged them to get married. He left a few days before the wedding was to take place. Rosario had her baby girl, Tatiana, and finished high school with a deep sense of shame that she hid well throughout her life. She became a yoga and gym instructor and eventually opened a small fitness business in a two-story house. They lived on the second floor.

Eventually, Tatiana went to college and became a psychology major. During her first term, she met Felipe, a medical school student from a middle-class family. While Felipe's father liked Tatiana very much, his mother was silently opposed to the relationship because of their class difference. Over the years, Tatiana worked hard to win Felipe's family's approval and was accepted by his mother and siblings. She learned their values and customs and was able to stay connected with them as well as her own family and community. It was as if she lived in two worlds, the humble, cozy, more open and simple world of her community, and the tighter, rule-bound world of Felipe's family, driven by a concern about what others would think ("el qué dirán").

While in her last year of college, Tatiana felt ill and went back home at a time when she was not expected. There she found one of her aunts in bed with another woman. She was shocked, and she froze in disbelief. She never said a word to anyone, but was greatly impacted in ways that she did not understand because this event reminded her of her own attraction to another girl when they were both in their teens. They had kissed. She then buried this memory and did not want to ever remember it. Although she had not been raised within a strict Catholic environment, she knew well that this was considered a sin and that her family would never regard same-sex relationships with kindness. She began to question herself, her worth, and her relationship with Felipe, but she stayed with him. She graduated and got a job and continued with life as usual for a while.

Although Felipe prided himself on being very liberal and somewhat of a bohemian, he was a goal-oriented individual who sought to become a well-known physician. He had planned to move to Canada to further his studies after finishing his residency in Santiago, and his plan involved taking Tatiana with him. However, Tatiana did not want to leave Chile. She did not see herself without her longtime friends, she knew little English, and she felt terrified to be alone and completely dependent on him in another country. After much back and forth, tears and arguments about his plans, and flaring up of old conflicts that they'd managed to keep aside for years, they broke up. He left, but they stayed connected as friends. After all, they had always been good pals.

Tatiana's life without Felipe left a strong vacuum. He had been her only serious and longtime boyfriend. At a time when most of her friends were getting married or making plans to do so, she sometimes felt like an outsider and wondered what her life would be. Nevertheless, she liked her new freedom and felt liberated from the expectation of having a family and settling into the role of a wife. She was outgoing and felt that her youth, energy, and curiosity would serve her well to meet new people and enjoy life. She met Ximena at a party through one of her friends. Like her, Ximena was outgoing and vibrant. Ximena was a social butterfly and had friends from all walks of life. Her looks and personality were like a magnet, which served her well in her job as an event planner. Ximena was bisexual, but this was only known within a small circle of trusted friends. After years of distance and silence from her parents, who disapproved of her "liberal" values and friends, Ximena had learned to navigate their social sensibilities and those of the many people she met in her personal and professional life. She was still closely connected to her younger brother, who had been a support for her during the good and the bad times.

Tatiana and Ximena fell for each other and began a two-year relationship in which they had to face the challenges of being a couple in a highly prejudiced and unsafe environment, in spite of the acceptance and support of many of Ximena's friends. Again, Tatiana learned to live in two worlds, the one she shared with her family, high school and college friends, and colleagues at her job, and that intense world of Ximena's, filled with social events and people from various regions within and beyond the country. They kept their homes separate and tried hard to keep their relationship hidden from their families and people who would not approve. Tatiana enjoyed exploring her new sense of self and chose to stay in the present because thinking about the future caused her great anxiety. She thought that she could never develop bridges between the various parts of her life.

Their relationship faced the hardest challenge when one of Ximena's boyfriends, Carlos, came back into her life. They had had a brief, emotionally abusive relationship, and he never came to terms with Ximena's decision to end it. Besides, he had relied on her financially and to develop his own event planning and catering business, and their paths crossed once in a while.

Carlos suspected that Ximena was attracted to women and found out that she was involved with Tatiana. He threatened to out them to their families and friends if Ximena did not loan him a large sum of money. Faced with his attempt to extort her, Ximena fought him and refused to give in. However, after many heated conversations and much conflict, he managed to shake their world upside down by taking money from them and letting Tatiana's family and other people know about their relationship. Tatiana's family members confronted her; she endured abusive comments and jokes and was almost raped by a man from her family's neighborhood. She had a nervous breakdown and almost lost her job.

When Felipe came back from Canada, Tatiana had been able to put her life back together and mend family relationships. Ximena was no longer in her life. Tatiana and Felipe dated again and decided to get married within a year. In the meantime, he was offered an exciting position in a hospital back in Canada and they decided to move there after the wedding. His visa did not allow her to work, but initially this did not matter because she planned to be a mother and stay at home for a few years. Eventually, they had two children and her time was devoted to their lives. Occasionally, they visited their families in Santiago. But life did not progress in a linear fashion. Over time, the relationship dried up, and they both had relationships outside the marriage. By the time Tatiana was in her mid-fortiess, her two adolescent daughters were finishing high school, she and Felipe were no longer together, and she had partnered with Diana.

Diana was a Colombian human rights activist who had to leave the country during Pastrana's government. She continued to be active during her exile and was later able to work in various parts of Central America and Colombia. Tatiana and Diana met through a mutual friend who helped Tatiana get a volunteer position as a way to begin the transition from homemaker to worker outside the home. Tatiana found a new path for her life in education and human rights, got a master's degree, and continued her involvement in human rights advocacy. Tatiana kept her relationship with Diana hidden from her family for a few years until she felt confident and economically independent enough to leave the marriage. One of her daughters inadvertently helped her when she mentioned in passing that she liked both girls and boys.

In one of their work-related trips to Colombia, Diana and Tatiana visited the southwestern region, including the departments of Cauca, Nariño, and Putumayo. Diana had been born in a small town in Cauca where Mestizos and Whites coexist with large populations of Indigenous peoples like Paeces and Guambianos and Afro-Colombians, among others. One evening during the intercultural festival celebrated in Pasto, Nariño's capital, where Indigenous peoples from all over Abya Yala (the Americas) met to share their wisdom and celebrate their traditions, Diana and Tatiana spent an evening with a small gathering of taitas (shamans), a local artist, a philosopher, and a handful of other visitors.

During the conversation, they learned that, with the Inca empire expansion, many communities might have been displaced and relocated far from their original lands and made servants of the empire. When the Spaniards arrived in this commerce-rich and highly populated region, they not only decimated the population with their diseases and brutality, but also with the help of the Inca's servant class and others who resented the Inca conquest. The Spaniards likely promised them land in return for helping them subjugate other Indigenous communities. What happened? As everywhere in the Americas, these promises were never kept. Over time, other bloodthirsty and greedy Spaniards, friars, Criollos, and Colonos (nonindigenous Whites) kept taking away their lands.

This southwestern region, mostly located in the Andes, has felt the impact of colonization from times immemorial, but traditional knowledge has been guarded, exercised, and sustained there. Cultural matrices continue to find expression through language, ritual, and connection to the land. Tatiana and Diana were there on a humanitarian mission to document human rights abuses perpetrated by the guerrillas and paramilitary on peasants and Indigenous groups. It seemed as if time passed in circles there, and land ownership conflicts repeated themselves generation after generation. How strange, they thought, that their own nationalities and heritage, and their personal struggles for *being* had brought them together across national, language, gender identity, and sexual orientation borders.

During part of their work there they stayed at the home of an Indigenous taita whose family had kept the knowledge of local healing traditions and medicinal plants. He was well known in some U.S. circles, and White Americans and Europeans traveled to visit his very humble home in Colombia to find help in meeting their spiritual and health needs. These seekers and travelers found ways to get to this remote place; they defied stereotypes about traveling to Colombia and left their comfortable and sometimes safe lives to visit a home in the midst of beautiful highlands, but with no heating system or hot water.

In Colombia, as in other parts of Latin America, Tatiana and Diana were a part of the large Mestizo population and the dominant culture because of their upbringing, ethnicity, gender, and class. Tatiana and Diana met Josh, a White gay man from the United States who had been going there for a while and had a close relationship with the taita and his family. Josh was very grateful for the healing he received there. He believed that this alternative form of medicine helped him overcome a major illness and serious relationship issues. Thus, he often brought expensive gifts to the taita, his family, and others in the community. In his eagerness to help, he often overstepped his boundaries and gave little thought to how his actions might have reflected a lack of awareness of his misuse of class and ethnic privilege as the host family almost immediately made efforts to serve him in any way they could. Tatiana and Diana found themselves in a conundrum when, on the one hand, Josh and other English-speaking visitors would joke and complain about how sexist the locals were, how awkward the local government was, how "all" young women got pregnant at a very young age, and how men drank and behaved like "machos," and could not understand why the host family would not use the household gifts he brought right away and kept using their old utensils. On the other hand, Tatiana and Diana also overheard some members of the host family discussing their prejudicial views and joking about same-sex relationships. Because they could converse with both the visitors and the host family and, to some extent, travel back and forth between their worlds, they found themselves in a very difficult border space.

The above cases illustrate how in these in-between spaces people have had to incorporate in their lives multiple knowledges, practices, and values that are not always coherent. As a result, they have developed the ability to see the world from the perspective of the dominant culture as well as from the perspectives of marginalized cultures. Geographical, relational, and psychological spaces characterized by this fluidity have been called *nepantla* in the work of Gloria Anzaldúa (1981, 1987, 2000, 2002). The experience of being pulled between realities or having to constantly negotiate multiple ways of being can be painful and transformative. Nepantla is also a process by which communities, families, and individuals "construct knowledge, identity, and reality, and explore how some of your/others' constructions violate other people's ways of knowing and living" (Anzaldúa, 2002). Nepantla can be, in addition, a space of hope and possibility.

While a text can never capture the richness and complexity of people's experiences, it is the medium that I have chosen to undertake the difficult task of moving back and forth from people's efforts to heal their present individual, relationship, and community issues to conceptualizations of history, social relationships, and healing. I wish there were a way to convey these ideas by integrating text, sounds, textures, and images to allow the reader to soften and/or intensify, change the pace, and create her/his own experience.

DECOLONIAL THOUGHT

Decolonial thought, according to the modernity/coloniality collective project and Chicana feminists, includes both theoretical positions and a critical intellectual project that should not be confused with postcolonial studies or with a critique of colonial practices. Its basic point of reference is a world system in which modernity began and evolved politically and economically in fifteenth-century Europe and then expanded throughout the world, hand-in-hand with the "discovery" of the "New World." One of its theses is that European colonial expansion connects many parts of the world, reaching a global scale and opening the possibility for examining local experiences in any region of the planet in the context of this world system. However, modernity did not reach all parts of the world in the same manner.

Modernity, understood as a civilizing project, a system of economic relationships, and a system for governing populations and mapping territories, created itself at the same time that many forms of knowledge, populations, subjectivities, and practices were constructed as being outside of itself. That which is "outside" of modernity is called by Walter Mignolo (2005) the "colonial difference," a privileged epistemological and political space from which one can construct projects that are an alternative to those which modernity produces.

Thus, when a group of Samoan, Maori, and Pakeha (White New Zealanders) developed an approach to healing families in New Zealand that was anchored in the values and traditions of their communities, and that took into account the destructive legacy of colonization, the notion of what needed to be healed changed, and other ways of addressing interpersonal problems emerged (Waldegrave & Tamasese, 1994).

Similarly, a Colombian family therapist, who defined issues of domestic violence within a larger context of economic and other forms of violence, adapted ideas and strategies from the family therapy field to the community's own vision and ways of relating; the healing processes that developed became something else—something outside the canon established by the disciplines and professions whose roots can be traced back to the European Enlightenment (Nensthiel, 2012). This therapist's standpoint was that of a Colombian Mestiza doing family and community work.

Likewise, when Rhea Almeida developed an approach that dealt with the interconnections of power, privilege, and oppression in family life, it made more sense to work within a collaborative framework, creating communities of support and accountability, than with individual families in isolation (Almeida, Dolan-Del Vecchio, & Parker, 2007). Her standpoint was that of a woman whose own long trajectory of migration journeys confronted her with the effects of ethnicity, class, gender, sexual orientation, ability, and religious preference in various social contexts.

Contemporary helping professions, such as counseling, counseling psychology, family therapy, and clinical psychology, have tremendously advanced our ways of addressing individual and interpersonal problems. They have contributed to redefining normalcy, integrating culture and social context in treatment, alleviating distress and maladjustment, and addressing normal developmental issues associated with physical, emotional, and mental problems. However, to the extent that these professions are embedded in systems of thought and practice that maintain ethnocentric foundations in regard to science, research, health, and models of practice, they will continue to have an oppressive impact, even if unintended, on some of the very people they aim to help.

Perhaps the time has come to examine how to decenter these cannons of practice in ways that will allow their coexistence with other knowledges and practices emerging from the colonial difference. I do not mean to suggest that anything deemed alternative (e.g., new age) is among the knowledges and practices that stem from the colonial difference. Neither should it be assumed that standards of practice and ethical principles guiding the welfare of those with whom we work are not of the utmost importance.

Prilleltensky and Nelson (2002) and Prilleltensky and Prilleltensky (2006) offered us a framework of interdependent values to uphold in the broad range of psychology and counseling and family therapy practices. These values include (a) self-determination, freedom, and personal growth; (b) health, caring, and compassion; (c) respect for diversity, collaboration, and democratic participation; (d) accountability and responsiveness to the common good; (e) support for community structures; and (f) social justice. Balancing these values while attending to the specifics of context and history is necessary when developing therapeutic practices that are relevant to many populations across the Americas—or Abya Yala, as the Kuna people call these lands.

In the following chapters, I invite readers to intuitively, experientially, and intellectually engage in the ideas presented, question them, and develop their own. The next chapter will delve into the underpinnings of the modernity/coloniality collective project. Its discussion will extend into the following chapter, which integrates Chicana feminist thinking and a framework for thinking about borderland experiences.

NOTE

1. This case was written by Logan Cohen, marriage and family therapist (MFT), and myself.

Chapter Two

A New Musical Score, a Horizon, and Possibilities for Meaning Making

A Decolonization Paradigm

I will introduce this chapter with a short story that occurred to me after having a conversation with a family therapist and taita (shaman) about his view that most people from the dominant culture in the South American countries he visited saw themselves as Westerners, yet they were living under conditions of colonization.

There was an old quirquincho (armadillo; from the Quechua khirkinchu) lying near some rocks somewhere in the Andes. She was listening to soft and musical sounds that the wind brought by going through the cracks of the rocks; with her eyes closed, she basked in the sweetness of these sounds and felt them throughout her shell. She also loved to wait till dawn to hear the frogs croaking in the swamps. As she listened to their songs, she immersed herself in their melodies but cried, wanting to be able to sing with such harmony. The frogs always let her know that she would never croak like them. One day, a man passed by with a couple of canaries. When the quirquincho heard them singing, she followed the man until she had a chance to ask them how to sing. She learned to listen to her own sounds, to trust her own knowledge, and to develop melodies that became a part of the Andean landscape. Who would have thought that a quirquincho could sing and maybe even dance one day?

In his introduction to *Interculturalidad, Descolonización del Estado y Conocimiento,* Walter Mignolo (2006) explained that decolonial thinking involves various narratives and ways of life, living, and doing that exist and develop "parallel and complementary to social movements that move along the edges and the margins of political and economic structures," and that become themselves as they detach from an image of a whole that makes us believe that there is literally no way out. The detachment that decolonial thinking promotes involves confidence that other worlds are possible (not a unique and new one that we believe may be the best, but other or different) and that these worlds are in the process of planetary construction (Mignolo, 2006, p. 10).

In this chapter, I will review the underpinnings of the modernity/coloniality collective project and a decolonization perspective, inclusive of standpoint and Chicana feminists' theories, to assist us in creating those new melodies that the quirquincho produced, that is, melodies that today fuse the Andean and African rhythms and instruments of our ancestors with those from other parts of the world, including Europe and Asia.

The modernity/coloniality collective project utilizes a paradigm rooted in Latin America that runs counter to such modernist narratives as Christianity, liberalism, and Marxism, and locates itself at the borders of these systems of thought. It reaches toward ways of thinking that are in contradistinction to Eurocentric philosophies (Escobar, 2007; Mignolo, 2005; Maldonado-Torres, 2005; Quijano, 2000b). The modernity/coloniality project has been nurtured by liberation theology and philosophy, critical theories of modernity and postmodernity, Chicana feminist theory, South Asian subaltern studies, and African philosophy, among others. This paradigm has recently been enriched by third-world feminist critiques (Lugones, 2003, 2005, 2010) and Grosfoguel's (2006, 2007) examination of epistemic privilege. Let us look at the following vignettes to ground these concepts in the everyday lives of Latino and Latin American families in South, Central, or North America, or Abya Yala[1] , as the Kunas refer to the whole of the American continent.

Ana Gonzalez is a single Latina working-class mother of two who lives in the New York-New Jersey metro area. Her daily routine involves waking up at 5:30 a.m. to get her children ready for school, dropping them at the bus stop, getting to work at 8:00 a.m. to labor at a factory until 5:30 p.m., with a half-hour break for lunch. Her children are picked up in the afternoon at the bus stop by her neighbor, and Ana takes them home by 7:00 p.m. During the next two hours, she helps them with homework, cooks dinner, and gets things ready for the next day. Ana works hard to provide for her children, hoping that their lives will be different than hers. However, she usually misses attending her children's back-to-school nights and parent-teacher conferences because she is completely dependent on her employment and has no flexibility to negotiate a different schedule.

Ana's brother, Mario, is serving jail time for his involvement in the selling of contraband. He is one of the many Latino prisoners who, as a group, make up one-third of federal prison inmates (Pew Institute, 2009) and are overrepresented in the U.S. jail system. He is housed in a private correctional facility where he can work for a very low minimum stipend due to his good behavior and no prior criminal history. Though he earns $1.25 an hour for an eight-hour workday manufacturing garments, the corporation that owns the prison, Corrections Corporation of America (CCA), receives billions in annual revenues from prison labor (Hammes-Garcia, 2004). Mario's wife and mother-in-law are now taking care of the three children.

Neither Ana nor Mario's children learn anything about their family's country of origin, Ecuador, except for what they sometimes hear at home. They have never visited the country. They understand Spanish but cannot speak or write it. In spite of the family's efforts to counteract the larger social milieu in which they live, they learn that they have an ethnicity (are unlike others), that they are dark, and that their phenotype does not conform to the ideal standard—that being of Latin American descent is not as valuable as having European ancestry. At the large and ethnically diverse public school they attend, they learn that children coalesce with their own ethnic group; if they have friends from other ethnic groups, they might have to explain why to their Latino peers.

This codification of differences around race is not a new experience for this family in the United States. It can be traced back to the Spaniards' invasion of today's Southern Abya Yala and the First Nations' holocaust. A key demarcation of difference between the conquerors and the conquered was that of "race," and it implied that there was a supposed biological structure that made some people naturally inferior to others. This demarcation is well and alive but has many forms and degrees of sophistication. For example, Ana's family migrated from the central highlands to the coastal city of Guayaquil, where they quickly learned that the local Montubios were different (read: superior) to Mestizos like them.

Marlen Gutierrez, a twenty-three-year-old female from a lower-middle-class family and student attending a prestigious college with sliding-scale tuition, travels to school by bus. The bus route takes her through areas of the city she lives in where she witnesses the pain of beggar adults and children, young girls at the doors of brothels, homeless dogs, and people selling food and contraband in the street to make a living. Those who have cars can take a route through the hills surrounding the city and never confront the sight of everyday pain in a country where 5 percent of the population owns 95 percent of the lands and wealth while everyone else scrambles for the leftovers.

As a psychology major, she is exposed to a curriculum that covers basic psychological processes (e.g., learning, cognition, emotion) and their application in areas including clinical, organizational, and educational psychology. The curriculum is based on a body of knowledge primarily produced in the United States and Europe, and the majority of authors are White males. Unless she takes an elective course that would specifically address other contents and authors, or undertakes a specialization in community psychology. Thus, the psychology that she will practice will be fundamentally shaped by Eurocentric ideas.

Marlen's brother, Fabio, used to work for a local security company. When a British private military (paramilitary) company reached out offering jobs in Iraq, he took a job with a very high salary. Fabio was able to provide for his parents and Marlen for a while. After graduation, Marlen gets a full-time, minimum-wage job with a managed care organization. She is trained to diagnose and develop behavioral programs for individuals with depressive and anxiety symptoms. Her family pressures her to get married and have a family; however, she is attracted to women and has a relationship with a college mate that she hides from her family. When Fabio returns from Iraq, he searches for jobs but remains unemployed. His plans to marry his girl-friend Alexandra and have a family are postponed.

Catalina Perry and Sebastian Pernaut, a married couple attending graduate school in Illinois, United States, found themselves expecting a child and are planning how to organize their new family and their studies. Catalina meets with her chemistry lab friend, Patricia, at a popular Mexican taco shop where they each look like and behave like any other White student. They are served by the dark-skinned, Spanish-speaking daughters of the Mexican owner's establishment. Catalina shares with Patricia her excitement and plans. Catalina and Sebastian's families are fully engaged in the welcoming of the baby and in helping the couple through this transition. The families have known each other for generations and treasure their migration histories to South America and their French and British heritage. Although Sebastian's family tried to persuade them to pursue graduate education in Europe, the couple chose to go to the United States to take advantage of the business and financial networks that Catalina's family has there.

Catalina was born in the United States, where her father brought the family for a few years to further his family's salmon export company, which is one of more than 900 medium-size Chilean companies that sell products to the United States. Bilateral agreements between the countries allow for mmore than a thousand Chilean professionals to enter the United States for work purposes each year. Catalina plans to take a term off from graduate school while Sebastian continues studying. Her parents will arrive a month before the baby's delivery and his parents will visit afterward. Their siblings will take turns visiting and helping them with the baby. The couple plans to travel to Santiago during winter break, which is summer in the southern hemisphere, to spend the holidays with family, baptize the baby, and look into bringing a nana (domestic servant) back to help them.

In each of these cases, access and opportunity—as well as likelihood to choose, achieve, and develop as a person, as a family, and in a trade or in a profession—are shaped by class, ethnicity, sexual orientation, gender identity, and ability. Although Ana and Mario Gonzalez and Catalina Perry and

Sebastian Pernaut have migration experiences involving the South and North of Abya Yala and even have knowledge of English and Spanish, their worlds are vastly different due to their historical classes and their ethnic ties to an ancestry that, over hundreds of years, developed both discourses and social structures to retain the differences that separate them today. Marlen Gutierrez does not even know that her ways of thinking, her professional identity, and even her own personal opinions are closer to those of a White, urban, middle-class woman from the United States than to a nana from Perú, Colombia, Ecuador, or Chile.

Ana, Mario, Marlen, Fabio, Catalina, and Sebastian's communities and families are embedded in asymmetrical relationship patterns driven by economic, political, and social forces. Although the everyday challenges and solutions these individuals face are not determined solely by these forces, they influence the individuals' participation in cultural identities and practices. For Ana, Mario, and the rest, their ways of thinking, behaving, and relating involve both their own agency and the hand of cards, so to speak, they each have to deal with at a given time.

The decolonization perspective articulated by the Latin American modernity/coloniality collective project and Chicana feminists, and the contributions from standpoint feminists, offer us a conceptual framework for interpreting and articulating how the world looks to some of us when we know, experience, speak, and imagine it while situated in the dwellings of double consciousness, border thinking, and subaltern epistemologies. The decolonization perspective also helps us orient ourselves toward resignifying the multiple overlapping and divergent but coexistent patterns of ethnicity, gender identity, race, sexual orientation, and epistemic and economic relationships with which we live (Grosfoguel, 2005).

COLONIALISM

The conquest and colonization of America was the formative moment in the creation of Europe's *other*; the point of origin of the capitalist world system, enabled by gold and silver from America; the origin of Europe's own concept of modernity (and of the first, Iberian, modernity, later eclipsed by the apogee of the second modernity); and the initiation point of Occidentalism as the overarching imaginary and the self-definition of the modern/colonial world system (Escobar, 2004).

Colonization has been a key constitutive factor in shaping our world. Abya Yala (Consejo Mundial de Pueblos Indígenas, 1977) was likely to have been populated by 60 to 110 million people before Columbus (Mann, 2005). In *Open Veins of Latin America*, Eduardo Galeano described the greed of the conquerors as follows:

America was the vast kingdom of the Devil, its redemption impossible or
doubtful; but the fanatical mission against the natives' heresy was mixed with
the fever that New World treasures stirred in the conquering hosts. Bernal Díaz
del Castillo, faithful comrade of Hernán Cortés in the conquest of México,
wrote that they had arrived in America "to serve God and His Majesty and also
to get riches." (1973, p. 13)

After contact with Europeans throughout the continent, First Nations people endured outbreaks of smallpox, measles, influenza, and other infectious
diseases, making conquest and colonization more viable (Mann, 2005).
Widespread violence, disease, and slavery were devastating to First Nations
peoples, who had complex societies and highly developed civilizations, like
those of the Maya, Inca, and Azteca (Bonfil Batalla, Dennis, 1996). They
became a commodity, and women and girls in particular were treated as
sexual objects (Wiesner-Hanks, 2000; Todorov, 1987). Thus, *mestizaje* resulted from the trade and rape of women, which over time was even regarded
as a desirable means to redeem one's lack of blood purity in what we, today,
call Latin America.

A person with First Nations ancestry could achieve personal and social
progress by mixing with Spaniards and Creoles to Whiten, although this was
not an option for those who had African ancestors (Castro-Gómez, 2007;
Rodriguez, 2007). At the time, these Mestizos were called *Ladinos* by Spaniards. However, De la Torre (2009) observed that the social, political, and
economic hierarchy was always clear: Spaniards or Portuguese first, then
Creoles, Mestizos, First Nations peoples, and Blacks.

Creoles, or Criollos, were people who saw themselves as of Spanish
origin but were born in the colonies. After independence from their European
masters, the Creole elites continued or developed new forms of violence
against First Nations peoples to appropriate their lands and labor. Examples
of the deterioration of First Nations peoples and the complexities that
evolved in their relationships with Ladinos and Criollos after the formation
of the Latin American republics can be found in the literary works of Jorge
Icaza (*Huasipungo*, 1999), Ciro Alegría (*El Mundo es Ancho y Ajeno,* 2003)
Miguel Ángel Asturias (*Hombres de Maíz,* 2005 [1949]), and Rosario Castellanos (*Balún Canán,* 2003), among others. Although some may consider this
historical legacy irrelevant, it has shaped the lives of all who inhabit these
lands; furthermore, life is not so different now for many people in today's
Abya Yala. Let us look again at Catalina and Sebastian's lives.

Catalina and Sebastian travel during Christmas to their native Chile to be
with family and baptize their baby, Carolina. Catalina's family always had a
female domestic employee or nana working inside the house; this employee
attended to the children and to general cleaning and cooking in the household. In addition, another employee was hired to work a couple of days a

week to finish these duties and to help with shopping and keeping up the garden.

Catalina's nana, Amanda, is a Mestiza born in the Araucanía region, the land of the Mapuche First Nations people. Lacking employment and hoping to give her children a better future, Amanda's mother had left her homeland with her two children and migrated to the capital. She worked as a nana for Catalina's great-grandmother and grandmother. Eventually, Amanda began working for the family.

Like her mother, Amanda earns a low salary with no benefits or social security. However, because this job pays better than a factory job and affords her a little more flexibility, she chooses to stay. Amanda grew up knowing her place in the society as a brown, Mestiza-looking woman with less than a high school education and no family and community connections to support her identity, development, and accomplishments in life. Like other nanas, Amanda has to wear a uniform that clearly identifies her as such. When she used to help her patrona, Catalina's mother, with Catalina and her siblings at the golf club, Amanda was not allowed to enter spaces reserved for members and guests only.

As a teenager Amanda had an unplanned pregnancy that turned into a miscarriage; she also had an abortion following her rape by one of Catalina's relative. The family quietly helped her find a place where it could be performed, and they paid for everything. Although Amanda does not complain about her working conditions and likes the family, she currently has no scheduled working hours, no holidays, and no rights that protect her from any kind of potential abuse by her employers. Catalina and Sebastian are considering taking Amanda to help them with Carolina or asking her to help them get one of her family members to do so.

According to a recent Chilean national survey addressing Indigenous and non-Indigenous women's opinions about the conditions of their livelihood (Humanas, 2011), 84 percent of all the women felt the most discriminated against in their work places; Indigenous women felt more discriminated against in their life, and in specific areas such as politics (99 percent) and the media (96 percent). The results indicate that the main problems the Indegenous women face involve poverty, lack of opportunity, and lack of recognition. Therefore, the overall legacy of racial discrimination and economic exploitation that usually includes lack of education, or a low-quality education, and lack of access to health services, persists today.

Though positive social and economic changes have occurred in the last five hundred years, the social and economic structures and discourses that maintain access, opportunity, and stability for some and not for others are still in place. Scholarly works addressing the complexities of race, class, and gender continue to document inequality among racial groups and between women and men (Bastos, 1998; Bengoa, 2000; Cirio, 2003; Wade, 2010; Winkler & Cueto, 2004).

A general understanding of colonialism is relevant to anyone working in a mental health field because, as Monk, Winslade, and Sinclair (2008) explained, it has influenced the entitlements that people claim, the privileges and lack of privileges that they may have, family composition, life expectations, and even how they respond to adversity. These authors affirmed that "the psychological effects of colonization that persist to this day cannot be fully understood by counselors and by their clients without taking account of the history of the cultural relationships reproduced by colonization" (p. 56).

In a similar vein, Duran, Firehammer, and Gonzalez (2008) insisted that therapists pay attention to how, in this age, colonization is accomplished not with guns and threats, but through people who change the hearts, minds, and spirits of others by promoting their own cultural belief systems. Therapists have the duty to avoid acts of colonization. Within the fields of psychology, counseling, social work, and family therapy, Martín-Baró (1982, 1990, 1994), Comaz-Díaz (2007), Duran and Duran (1995), Duran, (2006), and many others (Comaz-Díaz, Lykes, & Alarcón, 1998; McNeill & Cervantes, 2008; Rober & Seltzer, 2010) have discussed how colonization and its legacies must be attended to in the development of therapeutic practices that address social context in a life-affirming way.

According to the modernity/coloniality collective project (Escobar, 2001, 2003, 2004; Grosfoguel, 2005), *colonialism* refers to a form of political and judicial domination over the means of production, work, and livelihood that one population assumed over another through a historical period that can be marked as ending in 1824 with the independence battles that freed Latin America from Spain. These scholars have contend, however, that the end of colonialism, marked by the independence of the colonies beginning in the 1800s, did not end the power relationships that produce and legitimize oppressive differences between forms of knowledge, groups of people, and societies.

Peruvian sociologist Anibal Quijano (2000a, 2000b) asserted that a process based on the "knowledge of the other" has been extending oppression, for example, through institutions of education that reinforce the practice of studying others by inviting those others to contribute to their knowledge-building efforts while keeping their status in society marginalized and their contributions valued only when they become part of larger dominant discourses reinforcing the powers in place. Thus, colonial relationships persist, although mutated through discourses, symbols, and collective representations of social life about incommensurable differences that privilege some over others. The notions of race, gender identity, and culture are at the forefront of such discourses, establishing those who lack privileges as the other.

For example, Ana's parents were born in a country that could be considered politically independent since 1830. However, Ecuador, like most countries in the Caribbean and Central and South Abya Yala, has been under the economic and political yoke of the United States, the international banking community (the United States and Europe), and international corporations in various ways, even until today. Ecuador has a population of 13.8 million people; it is both geographically and ethnically diverse, and it has a relatively long, albeit unstable, experience with democratic rule. According to a report from the United Nations Development Programme (2008), despite a significant reduction in poverty in the last ten years, poverty and inequality are connected to gender, geography, and ethnicity, and persistent poverty encourages increased emigration.

As a family of humble origins from the highlands, with high school-level education, and limited access to credit, jobs, and education, Ana's family migrated to the United States in the 1970s with tourist visas; they stayed and worked their entire lives in manual and service occupations. Through the Immigration and Control Act of 1986, they became residents and, eventually, acquired citizenship. While Ana and Mario grew up having to negotiate their ethnic minority status at school, in the neighborhood, and eventually in their jobs, their parents had to do so to a lesser degree because their lives were organized mostly within the boundaries of the Latin American neighborhood where they settled.

As a heterosexual, able-bodied Latina of low socioeconomic status, Ana's path in life is typical of a woman from her generation and in her circumstances. She finished high school and entered the workforce to help her parents, got married in her early twenties to another Ecuadoran immigrant, and had two children. He became economically and emotionally abusive, was eventually unfaithful, and left the country, leaving her with the sole responsibility for raising the children. Ana is also mostly responsible for her aging parents' well-being.

She is the caretaker for the previous and the next generations. She is the culture bearer in the family, a typical role that women play in most cultures. In her job at the factory, she excels in her duties to counteract the racial prejudice that she experiences from supervisors and higher-level management. In spite of her achievements and resilience, Ana's life is intertwined with a longstanding historical legacy of institutionalized forms of sexism, racism, and classism that impacts her life in major ways.

COLONIZATION OF BEING

Mignolo (2005) and Maldonado-Torres (2005) used the term "colonization of being" to refer to the ideas and practices that have made particular groups of people invisible. This is clearly seen in the visual media and in mass marketing methods throughout history (e.g., portrayals of and references to the typical "American family" often exclude large sectors—usually those at the margins—of the population, for example, Latinos).[2] According to Mignolo, the colonization of being operates through conversion to the ideals of modernization and Western democracy.

The Creole-Mestizo elite, for example, elevates and follows Western European standards by promoting lighter-skinned people in the media; and by borrowing flawed for-profit models of health management that have proven ill-equipped to serve people (for example, Colombia used the U.S. for-profit healthcare model as the template for its current health managedcare system, with disastrous consequences) (Jasso-Aguilar, Waitzkin, & Landwehr, 2004). Another powerful instrument of conversion involves importing academic standards based on hierarchical, exclusionary systems of power, which requires future professors to pursue studies typically in Europe and North America and to then implement the very knowledges and practices that came about from the epistemic expansion of the Western world (Dowling, 2008).

COLONIALITY

According to Mignolo (2000a, 2000b, 2005), *coloniality* refers to the systemic suppression of subordinated cultures and knowledges by the dominant Eurocentric paradigm of modernity, and the emergence of knowledges and practices resulting from this experience. It addresses the "power differential, not only in the accumulation of riches and military technologies of death but in the control of the very conception of life, of economy, of human being and labor" (p. 53). The emergence of knowledges and practices at the margins has the potential to engender distinct alternatives, thereby fostering a pluriverse of cultural configurations.

Mignolo articulated two interrelated aspects of the coloniality of being: the systemic suppression of local knowledges and the emergence of alternative knowledges resulting from this oppressive experience. Marlen's case offers an illustration of the former in a secular higher education context. Throughout her elementary, high school, and college education, she barely learned that First Nations peoples and people of African descent existed in her native country and that there were lively small communities there in contemporary times. In addition, any knowledge or practice considered part of that country's popular knowledge was systematically undermined and dismissed as fetishizing, primitive, and superstitious. The history lessons she received barely mentioned the achievements and contributions of ancestors other than Criollos. In spite of their mixed ethnic heritage, Marlen's family was never connected to anything related to First Nations customs, practices, or rituals. They were mostly connected to their lower-middle-class cultural milieu in which there is a legacy of hybrid traditions involving herbal medicine and curanderismo. However, the more she consumed Western psychology knowledge in college, the more removed she became from anything that had to do with her local upbringing and culture.

Regarding the emergence of alternative knowledges, there is enormous variation in knowledges of health. For example, throughout Abya Yala, there exists a rich reservoir of knowledges about well-being, including knowledge about the use of myriad indigenous plants and practices that involve developing an awareness of one's actions and the impact that those actions have on others (Ascani & Smith, 2008; McNeill, Esquivel, Carrasco, & Mendoza, 2008). For example, in their book *Curandero Conversations*, Zavaleta, Salinas, and Sams (2009) explained that *curanderismo* is a term used first by anthropologists to describe the healing systems of people. The authors documented many Mexican curanderismo practices in use today.

Another example of the use of First Nations healing practices involves yajé or ayahuasca ceremonies. Yajé is a brew that has been used for ritual and healing purposes in the Amazon basin since pre-Colombian times, and it is integral to ritual practices, myths, cosmologies, art, music, and most other aspects of cultural life (Gow, 1994; Reichel-Dolmatoff, 1997). However, its use for medicinal and spiritual purposes has grown beyond the Amazon borders. In Colombia, local groups host taitas (First Nations shamans), who administer this medicine in ceremonies, following traditional indigenous protocols that are attended by people of all socioeconomic classes and ages (Uribe, 2008).

In Peruvian contexts, it is called ayahuasca, and outside indigenous contexts, it is integral to a broader practice of plant-based ethnomedicine (Luna, 1986). It is consumed in religious contexts in Brazil and the United States (e.g., Santo Daime and União do Vegetal); indigenous-style ayahuasca healing ceremonies are conducted in the Amazon, all over Abya Yala, Europe, Australia, and New Zealand, and some parts of Asia (Dobkin de Rios & Rumrill, 2008); and it is privately consumed by people who buy the dried plant material through the Internet (Halpern & Pope, 2001). The brew is typically prepared from two plants, *Banisteriopsis caapi* and *Psychotria viridis*, which contain harmala alkaloids and dimethyltryptamine (DMT). Its ceremonial use produces a biochemical synergy resulting in profound idiosyncratic psychoactive effects (Shanon, 2002).

Although it is not within the scope of this chapter to address the history and contemporary issues related to the use of DMT, it is worth noting two issues that reflect the continued challenges that indigenous healing practices present to our contemporary "modern" world. First is the dilemma that Western liberal democratic states have faced while trying to simultaneously uphold religious freedom, and punitive "drug" control laws that deem DMT a controlled substance. Second is the ways in which cultural globalization provides opportunities for First Nations peoples to obtain recognition, acceptance, and empowerment (Tupper, 2009).

Based on the notion of subaltern knowledge, introduced by Guha (1993) and Prakash (1999), and Bhabha's (1994a) ideas on borders and spaces of knowledge production and subordination, Mignolo (2005, 2009a) further developed the idea of decentering knowledge construction by multiplying the loci of enunciation by incorporating the point of view of subordinate groups at any colonial moment from the 16th century to the present. Thus, the emergence of alternative knowledges resulting from the oppressive experience of coloniality is the conceptual location for border thinking. In Mignolo's view, border thinking emerges from the fissures between the ways in which modernity describes the world, and the colonial histories, memories, and experiences of wounded subordinate groups.

As Escobar (2003) stated, "The conquest and colonization of America is the formative moment in the creation of Europe's Other. This is the marker that crystallizes binaries such as subject/object, self/other, nature/culture into a system of hierarchical classification of people and nature" (p. 60). Feminists have explained that gender and racialization processes are patriarchal and colonial tools of "otherization" that have justified violence toward women and people of Color. So while in a patriarchal system the notion of "woman" is constructed as other and marginal and secondary to man, who is at the center (Beauvoir, 1970), in a Eurocentric system, people of Color are constructed as other, marginal, and secondary to White people who are at the center (Dussel, 1992). When race and gender are seen in relation to each other, along with other dimensions such as sexual orientation and class, a "matrix of domination" (Collins, 1998) emerges, highlighting how interweaving systems simultaneously impact a family.

Thus, when we develop therapeutic models explicitly based on differences that construct the "other," we assist in reinforcing the dialectical connectedness of the privileged self who studies and helps the other, and the marginal other who is studied and intervened with by the members of the dominant group. The invisibility of this dialectical connection is embedded within White privilege and thus reinforces the explicit decentering of equity through barricades of economic, social, and political access. To "other" someone is dehumanizing and contributes to delegitimizing their culture as inferior, thereby facilitating, even justifying, their oppression (Almeida, Hernández-Wolfe, & Tubbs, 2011). Uruguayan writer Eduardo Galeano (2000) described this process of delegitimization by pointing to the way dominant cultures understand those whom they have converted into an other as those who do not speak a language but a dialect, do crafts but not art, and who have a folklore but not a culture.

"THE HUBRIS OF THE ZERO POINT"

Colombian philosopher Santiago Castro-Gómez (2010) coined the term "the hubris of the zero point" to refer to the knowledge of the observer who cannot be observed. This is the foundation of the notion of objectivity and the foundation of today's social science. In his book, *La Hybris del Punto Cero: Ciencia, Raza e Ilustración en la Nueva Granada (1750–1816)*, Castro-Gómez argued that European philosophers such as David Hume, Immanuel Kant, and John Smith, whose seminal works comprise the foundation for the social sciences, constructed a discourse in which the peoples colonized by Europe were characterized as less developed and their ideas as primitive; at the same time, these philosophers praised the market economy, political institutions, and science conceived by the Enlightenment as the most advanced stage of humanity's development.

Castro-Gómez discussed Edward Said's (1978) analysis of modern colonialism, in which domination by force is not the only method of domination; another method is discourse about the other embedded within the everyday lives of both the colonizers and colonized. According to Castro-Gomez, studying the relationships between the Enlightenment, colonialism, and social science from Latin America sheds new light on Said's analysis in *Orientalism*. Castro-Gómez asserted that Whiteness was the first cultural and geographical imaginary of the world-system from which the ethnic division of labor and the transfer of capital and raw material was globally legitimized. He addressed the question of how "America" is at the center of European Enlightenment discourse and how it was read, translated, and enunciated in the New Granada (today's Venezuela, Colombia, and Ecuador) from a philosophical perspective.

His hypothesis is that Creole thinkers translated and enunciated this discourse without attending to their own cultural, historical, and ethnic location as a result of their belief in being "limpios de sangre" (of clean blood). They constructed the idea of having clean blood and continued a tradition of racist European ideology and used it to elevate themselves over everyone else born in Abya Yala. Thus, they positioned themselves as the dominant group vis-à-vis the other: Mestizos, First Nations peoples, peoples of African descent, and the combinations of these groups. The Creole elite who controlled access to education appropriated the Enlightenment's discourse of the social sciences to differentiate the knowledge they possessed from local and popular knowledges, thus demarcating further distinctions between social classes.

His work helps us understand how such an ethnically diverse region with the largest population of Mestizos developed a social representation of the other along similar lines to those established by Europeans earlier and in other parts of the world. Castro-Gómez (2007) explained:

What the Enlightenment proposed was to legitimate, by way of science, the establishment of disciplinary apparatuses that permitted the normalization of bodies and minds to orient them toward productive work. But it is precisely in the enlightened project of normalization where colonialism fits so well. Constructing the profile of the "normal" subject that capitalism needed (White, male, owner, worker, heterosexual, etc.) necessarily required the image of an "other" located in the exteriority of European space. The identity of the bourgeois subject in the seventeenth century is constructed in opposition to the images of "savages" who lived in America. (p. 429)

Let us look at an illustration of how Creoles positioned themselves as the dominant group vis-à-vis the other groups in Argentina. Buenos Aires and Montevideo were the most important ports in that part of the Atlantic Ocean and became the entryway of African slaves that populated the interior of the continent. Most of the Africans who populated Chile, Perú, Uruguay, and Argentina came from the regions that we know today as Angola and the Congo and spoke Bantú languages. While in the 1778 census the Black population was robust (e.g., Tucumán, 42 percent; Santiago del Estero, 54 percent; en Catamarca, 5 percent; Salta, 46 percent; en Córdoba, el 44 percent; en Mendoza, el 24 percent), throughout the 19th century there was a continued decrease until, at the end of the century, there was a massive influx of European immigrants (Bello & Rangel, 2002; Cirio, 2003; Rotker, 1999; Stubbs & Reyes, 2006). Rotker (1999) explained that the population declined but did not extinguish. However, they disappeared from the official census, and it is possible that the traditions and identity characteristics that held their communities together may have become less powerful over time.

Although Afro-Argentinians are alive and vibrant today, since the 1780s the Argentinian elite and the various waves of European immigrants made their Black population invisible. A 2005 pilot study surveying the presence of African descendants in two neighborhoods, one located in Buenos Aires, and the other in Santa Fé, revealed that 3 percent of the population knew about their African ancestors (Stubbs & Reyes, 2006). Like their counterparts in other parts of South Abya Yala, the state assumed its mission to Whiten the population as a prerequisite for the development and progress of the territory, using the promotion, from the constitution, of the White European population, the restriction of African or Asian immigration, and also to the denial of Black reality in the country (Chambers, 2003; Hofbauer, 2003; Loveman & Muniz, 2007; Loveman, 2009; Schaefer, 2008; Wade, 2008).

STANDPOINT EPISTEMOLOGY

Feminist scholars (Alarcón, 1990; Anzaldúa 1987, 1997, 2000; Collins, 1986, 1998; Haraway, 1988; Harding, 2003, 2008; Lugones, 2003; Sandoval,

2001; Moraga, 2011; Pérez, 2003; Wiley, 2001) have reminded us that we always speak from a particular location within power structures. Nobody escapes the class, sexual, gender, spiritual, linguistic, geographical, and racial hierarchies of the "modern/colonial capitalist/patriarchal" world-system. Specifically, feminist standpoint theory states that social location systematically influences our experiences, shaping and limiting what we know. Thus, what one can know is influenced by the kind of experiences one has; what we know is learned and known from a particular standpoint. Knowledge is embodied rather than acquired through a universal, disembodied, rational mind. Social inequalities generate distinctive accounts of nature, and social relationships and inequalities of different social groups create differences in their standpoints.

A standpoint is not a perspective but a critical reflection on the ways in which power structures and social location influence what and how we know. Harding (2004) defined standpoints as distinctive insights about how hierarchical social structures work, and Wylie (2003) defined a standpoint as "a critical consciousness about the nature of our social location and the difference it makes epistemically" (p. 31). Standpoint epistemology takes a step further: the analysis of the hubris of the zero. The hubris of the zero point makes visible that, in Western philosophy and sciences, the subject that speaks is always hidden from the analysis under the guise of objectivity. Thus, there is a claim to a truthful universal knowledge that conceals the geographical, political, social, and epistemic location of knowledge production. Standpoint epistemology articulates the ways in which knowledge production is shaped by social location.

There are several aspects of standpoint epistemology that deserve our attention: It is a form of knowledge that is primarily achieved collectively; it involves a commitment to making visible the ways in which social location shapes and limits scientific inquiry; and it advocates for the equitable inclusion and participation of members of marginalized communities in the process of knowledge construction (Inteman, 2010). According to standpoint epistemology, critical consciousness about knowledge and power is achieved by communities. While individuals may contribute to the accomplishment of critical consciousness within an epistemic community in different ways, the idea is that this is a social epistemology. For example, individual people of Color in the United States who were regularly stopped by the police and often were mistreated or even abused without any apparent reason may not have seen this experience as an expression of racism, and may have doubted how prevalent such mistreatment was in some states. Only when these experiences are articulated within communities of concerned individuals does there emerge a questioning of the status quo, practices of resistance, accountability, and policy change.

For example, Juan, a medical student attending a mid-Atlantic prestigious university, went to a relative's funeral in New Jersey. On the trip from the cemetery to his aunt's house, he and his family were stopped for speeding while driving 60 miles per hour in a 55-mile-per-hour zone. The group was forced to stand on the road in the rain for an extended period of time while the police searched the car. Civil lawsuits brought about an investigation by the Department of Justice into the activities of the New Jersey state police in 1998. It was found that there was a consistent pattern of racial profiling in motor vehicle stops along the New Jersey Turnpike.

According to a report from the U.S. Department of Justice (2000), Black drivers, who accounted for 17 percent of the state's population, made up 70 percent of drivers who were searched and had a 28.4 percent chance of carrying contraband. In contrast, White drivers had a 28.8 percent chance of carrying contraband and were searched far less often. Thus, as a group, Latinos were able to see the patterns of this form of racism and its effects.

Standpoint epistemology also involves mapping the "practices of power, the ways the dominant institutions and their conceptual frameworks create and maintain oppressive relations" (Harding, 2004, p. 31). It takes an ethical and political stance in rejecting the idea of science as a "value-free" enterprise, and in examining power relations, institutions, policies, practices, methodologies, and technologies that maintain oppression, in order to question, change, or abolish them.

For example, Maori scholar Linda Tuhiwai Smith (1999) explained that Western research brings with it a particular set of values and conceptualizations of time, space, subjectivity, gender relations, and knowledge that influence the gaze of the researcher. Accordingly, research on Indigenous peoples in the majority of cases has involved the extraction of knowledge for the benefit of the Western researcher and Western science. This knowledge has produced a wide range of negative consequences for Indigenous peoples, such as having their social and spiritual worlds explored, measured, and even appropriated.

In addition, those who have experiences of marginalization in one or more areas (Collins, 1998; Wylie, 2003) have special insights resulting from their having to learn the ways, values, and practices of dominant groups in addition to those of their own group. The experiences and knowledge generated from inhabiting spaces of marginalization often require that one learns well the practices and knowledge of dominant groups. The new knowledge generated from the marginalized standpoint regarding dominant practices and groups may help serve both those in dominant and marginalized positions. These new perspectives should be considered when taking into account the fluidity of social locations and without presupposing an essentialist definition of the social categories by which standpoints are characterized.

Finally, one should not assume that standpoints of the oppressed are automatically epistemically advantaged (Wylie, 2003), but that for this knowledge and contribution to be truly valued and articulated with the rigors of other bodies of knowledge, "there must be some sort of equality of intellectual authority and uptake of criticism."

DECOLONIZATION

Mignolo (2011) invited us to consider decolonial thinking as a critical theory and "the de-colonial option as a specific orientation of doing." We will examine and illustrate the following concepts to differentiate what these scholars mean by *decolonization*, including colonialism, coloniality, colonization of being, and the hubris of the zero point.

The experience of coloniality is a sine qua non for decolonization. From the perspective of the modernity/coloniality collective project, decoloniality must be thought of from the epistemological and political space of the "colonial difference" (Quijano, 2000a) or the "colonial wound"—that is, the experiences and subjectivities of the damned of the earth, of the victims of modernity. The point is not to adopt an anticolonial or anti-European stance, as it must be recognized that we speak from the perspective of the colonial wound, which was itself created by coloniality; we inevitably draw on knowledge produced from the other side of modernity, and cannot pretend disingenuously to be dislocated from that modernity.

Decoloniality refers to the processes through which people who are socially, politically, and geographically outside of hegemonic structures resist the rules and racialized hierarchies within which they are confined. This process is also about developing ways of being, knowing, doing, and relating that affirm knowledges and practices at the margins that have the potential to engender distinct, articulate alternatives to dominant practices.

Feminist queer Chicana scholar Emma Pérez (1999, 2003) has spoken of the decolonial imaginary as a space in between, where systems of domination are negotiated, and a space to inhabit and hold while at the same time challenging those systems. Pérez (1999) explained that social positioning should not be read as a binary describing, on one end, oppression and victimization and, on the other, privilege and perpetration. She insisted that multiple social positions are always at work, and this creates a liminal identity in which "one negotiates within the imaginary to a decolonizing otherness where all identities are at work in one way or another" (p. 7).

Escobar (2001, 2004) characterized decolonization as thinking through and from the practices of subaltern groups in contrast to the hegemonic, universalist epistemology from the perspective typical of a person having a White male body and located in Christian Europe and the United States.

Other authors (Quijano, 2000a, 2000b; Mignolo, 2009) have argued for an epistemological detachment or delinking from Eurocentric ways of thinking. Mignolo (2009) named this detachment "epistemic disobedience." Decolonial thinking requires that this detachment be from the global hegemony of the knowledge model that represents the local European historical experience at epistemological and political levels. However, the modernity/coloniality collective project's decolonization proposal is still influenced by the same theories and epistemologies that it criticizes. This proposal offers us a way to subversively reorient traditional theoretical frameworks into a deep questioning of ourselves.

Decolonial thinking is distinct from other critical projects in that it takes root at the colonies and excolonies in accordance with "an-other epistemology" and seeks a change in content, and in the limits and conditions of conversations (Mignolo, 2006). The project occupies itself with unearthing and articulating alternative ways of thinking from its dwellings in double consciousness, Mestiza consciousness, border thinking, and subaltern epistemologies.

Pérez (1999) distinguished between the colonial imaginary, that cognitive system that supports and rationalizes the continuing colonial systems, and the decolonial imaginary, which allows one to conceive of new possibilities, new categories, and social locations outside of the imposed and normalized colonial logics. She pointed out that even the colonized embody and are constrained by the colonial imaginary. In the following example of a therapeutic intervention using a perspective that integrates standpoint epistemology and a liberation-based healing framework for practice, I illustrate how we can think outside the traditional box of mental health and create other ways of healing.

A PRACTICAL ILLUSTRATION

The following case study recently published by Almeida, Hernández-Wolfe, and Tubbs (2011, pp. 50–51)[3], illustrates a community-based healing model using three family processes: critical consciousness, empowerment, and accountability. At its core, the model is an analysis of power, privilege, and intersectionality, and it will be further examined in chapter 5. For now, let us look at this community-based intervention.

Ishmael, an eighteen-year-old African American young man, was a part of a therapy program for youth on probation.[4] His mother was serving time for drug charges, his father was serving life for armed robbery, and he had no grandparents or relatives around. He was raised by his elderly godmother, who had less than a high school education and was receiving governmental assistance. Although she offered him a nurturing environment throughout his childhood, he, like many other adolescents, faced many challenges around gang initiation, drugs, and early fatherhood during his junior year in high school. He was referred to Affinity Counseling Center (ACC) where he entered a therapeutic community that offered him a way to understand and name the ways in which his life, and the lives of many in his close circle, were largely shaped by categories such as race, class, gender, sexual orientation, ability, religion, and other markers through a process of building critical consciousness. Many gang members had been court ordered to this center because of their repeated involvement with the criminal justice system, including many who had grown up with him and attended the same schools.

Ishmael was confronted by structural barriers to getting an education and a lack of social capital that could mitigate some of these barriers. Due to the enormous number of teens with complex difficulties in his school district, teachers were overwhelmed and often had limited expectations for their students. At Affinity Counseling, a therapeutic community embraced him with stand-in parents, elders from his community, peers who shared lived experiences, therapists, and activists. This healing community allowed him to process and reconsider many typical challenges facing teens in his circumstances.

As therapy progressed, Ishmael considered attending college and was later accepted at a local university. Therapists supported his dream by partnering with community activists/allies and clients who acted as mentors. But his dream of college entrance came with newly discovered barriers. He learned that entry into college did not entitle him to secure financial aid because, in the United States, student loans—state and federal—require a cosigner. The college that accepted him offered no financial options for this young man who wanted and deserved to break free from the cycle of poverty that had trapped his parents and many others in his community. Allies from a Baptist church offered to cosign on his behalf, with the condition that he attend a few church gatherings, but Ishmael was Muslim and was unwilling to accept an offer that involved worshiping another god.

The therapeutic community turned to a network of community allies who focus on justice through praxis and partner with them on a range of community-building/therapeutic initiatives. The Alliance for Racial and Social Justice (ARSJ), a group that engages in civic initiatives in which they lend their privilege and unearned benefits to those with disadvantages, agreed to research the case and eventually chose to support Ishmael's college dream by offering to cosign the loans.

Since they are an activist organization, not a philanthropic organization, it was important that Ishmael engage with them in activist projects. They invited Ishmael to participate in a range of community-building projects, including voter registration and Court Watch. These initiatives were designed to reinscribe the visibility of disaffected youth and to legitimize their presence within their own communities. This transformative endeavor facilitated Ishmael's reclaiming of his community as a contributing citizen, a milestone critical to his college launching. He was excited to be part of the process of restoring his overpoliced and disenfranchised community to its citizens. He also accepted an invitation to participate with ARSJ and present at the White Privilege Conference. He became a co-trainer on dismantling White privilege, reporting about those with collective disadvantages and expanding communities of resistance. All of these community-based assets became part of his social and cultural capital.

The day before he left for college, ARSJ, Affinity Counseling, and the Institute for Family Services (IFS) planned a celebratory ritual of his launching. Ishmael was embraced by a circle of mentors, community allies, clients with diverse problems from multiple backgrounds, and therapists. In the circle, he provided the final signature to the completed loan application and was presented with numerous gifts for his dorm room. Ishmael gave out thank-you cards to everyone, and, struggling to hold back tears, told the group, "I never had any family, and you are not even my family, but I see what family looks like."

As the celebration continued, members from ARSJ, as well as diverse members of the circle, both allies and clients, offered numerous reflections, such as the following: "Ellen and I are really proud of your perseverance throughout this past year and your sense of hope and even when every system around you seemed to shut you out"; "Ishmael, you have spent quite a bit of time in my home so you know that even as a White woman, I am a single GLBT parent and my 13-year-old is constantly having my lifestyle challenged by her friends' parents. I would never have survived financially, however, in spite of my college education, if it were not for my parents' consistent economic support. I think that legacy is often not spoken openly about."

The African American allies, members of the Baptist church, initially struggled with the fact that Ishmael turned down their offer to attend a few Sunday gatherings in exchange for the funding the church could offer him. They argued that even though he might today identify as Muslim, the African American community had a long tradition of participating in the Baptist faith. They had difficulty dialoging around the issue of difference within group and within faith. They also had difficulty grappling with the construct of privilege and power from their religious stance, although they were, in the end, able to come to terms with understanding the potential loss of a child from their community due to an assumption of identity/politics/cultural/religious homogeneity. After numerous conversations, the pastor and church committees decided to appoint a special committee that would, in the future, handle the dilemma that Ishmael handed them. They decided that a young

Black man trying to go to college against all odds must receive whatever aid they could offer, and his religious preference ought not to be a barrier.

SUMMARY

In this chapter I examined the underpinnings of the modernity/coloniality project and reviewed the following key concepts: colonialism, coloniality, the hubris of the zero point, and decolonization. The systemic suppression of subordinated cultures/ways of knowing (coloniality) is perpetuated through a dominant Eurocentric paradigm of modernity, and it comprises two key interrelated aspects: the continuous marginalization of local knowledges, and the unfolding of alternative practices and ways of knowing that endure and develop from this marginalization. Therapeutic models that are grounded in Eurocentered ways of healing perpetuate oppressive perspectives that reinforce coloniality. I discussed how they relate to standpoint epistemology and explained how we always speak from a particular social location, which is embedded within interwoven power structures, and how the hubris of the zero point has been used to sell and sustain the idea that science is "value free." Finally, I offered Ishmael's case as an example of another way to think about therapy and therapeutic interventions. If the reader is interested in using this material for further reflection, I provide a set of open-ended questions for dialogue in the Appendix. In the next chapter I will discuss the borderlands perspective and the notions of nepantla, intersectionality, and social and epistemic location.

NOTES

1. Abya Yala is the name that the Kuna people give to this content to mean "continent of life."
2. This is beginning to change in the United States due to the efforts of Black advertising entrepreneurs who have challenged the status quo of marketing only to White audiences.
3. Excerpts from this case have been reprinted here with permission from *The International Journal of Narrative Therapy and Community Work*, Dulwich Centre Publications, www.dulwichcentre.com.au.
4. Affinity Counseling Center (ACC), the Institute for Family Services (IFS), and the Alliance for Racial and Social Justice (ARSJ) collaborated to assist Ishmael.

Chapter Three

Nepantla

A Borderland Epistemology

Soy un amasamiento, I am an act of kneading, of uniting and joining that not only has produced both a creature of darkness and a creature of light, but also a creature that questions the definitions of light and dark and gives them new meanings.

We are the people who leap in the dark, we are the people on the knees of the gods. In our very flesh, (r)evolution works out the clash of cultures. It makes us crazy constantly, but if the center holds, we've made some kind of evolutionary step forward. Nuestra alma el trabajo, the opus, the great alchemical work; spiritual mestizaje, a "morphogenesis," an inevitable unfolding. We have become the quickening serpent movement.

—Gloria Anzaldúa, 1987, p. 103

In this chapter, I advance some ideas on decolonization by discussing my understanding of key concepts in Gloria Anzaldúa's work, consistent with thinking of Latin@s within the colonial history of Abya Yala. In addition, I integrate Maria Lugones's critique of and contributions to the modernity/coloniality project paradigm (1992, 2010) and Ramón Grosfoguel's distinct views on transnational feminisms (2006, 2012).

My working thesis is as follows: There are two interrelated aspects of the coloniality of being: the systemic suppression of local knowledges and the emergence of alternative knowledges resulting from this oppressive experience. Nepantla offers the possibility for these alternative knowledges to emerge and develop (Migonolo, 2011). This framework has much to contribute to the models, language, and practices that we call mental health, and to family and other therapies. I explore nepantla as a concept to anchor a discussion accompanied by (a) differentiating identity politics from epistemic and ethical projects that are grounded in subaltern identities and (b) understanding and articulating the ways in which gender identities, class, race, sexual orientation, and ability intersect and make visible not only multiple and complex oppressions within and between groups but also borderland spaces.

My personal, primary frame of reference is that of someone who inhabits the borderlands of bilinguality, binationality, and interculturality. This frame of reference involves an understanding of how knowledge and subjectivity are intertwined with modernity/coloniality, and what the constructing of knowledges and family therapy and other mental health practices in the borderlands can offer us in opening other paths of healing. I invite family therapists and others in the mental health fields to look into what other disciplines can offer and to consider the cross-fertilization of our practices.

ABOUT GLORIA ANZALDÚA

Gloria Anzaldúa was a Chicana, lesbian, feminist, Tejana patlache poet, writer, and cultural theorist born to field-worker parents. She began laboring with her parents and siblings at age eleven, and when her father died three years later, she had to continue working at the fields throughout high school and college. She won numerous awards for her writings, such as the Lambda Lesbian Small Book Press Award for *Haciendo Cara* (1990) and the Before Columbus Foundation American Book Award for *This Bridge Called My Back* (1997). Her book *Borderlands/La Frontera* (1987) was selected by the Library Journal as one of the thirty-eight Best Books of 1987. In her writing she used a unique blend of languages, including Spanish, English, and Nahualt. Anzaldúa wrote in "Spanglish," inviting the reader to experience what she experienced throughout her life in a land where non-English speakers were shunned and punished (University of Minnesota, 2012).

In addition, her work is grounded in her body and is connected physically and metaphorically to gender identity, sexual orientation, race, and class, and dialectic relationships between these and the self. She conceptualized pain as recursive vulnerability, necessary for personal and social transformation, and used her body as a means to embody geographical, cultural, and psychological borders as well as spiritual animal symbols. She did what the scholars from the modernity/coloniality collective project have not dared to do yet, that is, to make visible her own personal experience and use it to articulate her thinking. Her teoría insisted upon locating it in the body; hers was an embodied voice.

I believe that a decolonizing framework must be anchored in the reality inherent in multiple subjectivities and an embodied voice. Some male authors in the modernity/coloniality collective project (e.g., Escobar, 2003) identified a need for female and queer voices to emerge and be heard. However, this is no excuse for their not addressing the material and multiple other consequences of their male—and other kinds of—privilege in the nation states of Abya Yala. While Mignolo and Tostlanova (2006) have written about Anzaldúa's unique perspective and contribution to a decolonizing paradigm, they have not written about their views in ways that make visible their own social locations.

NEPANTLA: A BORDERLAND EPISTEMOLOGY

In her provocative preface to *Borderlands/La Frontera,* Gloria Anzaldúa (1987) introduced a discourse of people who live between different worlds and whose social conditions involve hybrid identities:

> The actual physical borderland that I'm dealing with in this book is the Texas-U.S. Southwest/Mexican border. The psychological borderlands, the sexual borderlands, and the spiritual borderlands are not particular to the Southwest. In fact, the Borderlands are physically present wherever two or more cultures edge each other, where people of different races occupy the same territory, where under, lower, middle and upper classes touch, where the space between two individuals shrinks with intimacy. (Anzaldúa, 1987, p. 19)

First, she referred to a geographic borderland that is a site and a symbol of great violence from the U.S. government and groups of U.S. citizens toward peoples coming from the South of Abya Yala, especially those who are dark-skinned. It also evokes asymmetries in labor division, and in concrete historical and material social conditions. Then she referred to other borderlands involving sexual orientation, class, gender, and race, which are as material as the geographical borderland, but encompass experiences that inform and transform each other. However, the idea is not to essentialize the cultures that meet at the borders or to homogenize borders as if there were only one border culture, identity, or even process of hybridization.

According to Anzaldúa (1987), the borderlands are the places in between, the spaces in which border knowledge and border identities are constructed; the gaps, fissures, and silences of hegemonic narratives (Rosaldo, 2008); and the overlapping border spaces and cultural representations that those who inhabit these spaces negotiate in order to exercise personal and collective agency (Lugones, 2005, 2007). The borderland concept is transnational and can be applied to the multiplicity of borders present in Abya Yala and is consistent with Lionnet and Shih's (2005) view of the transnational "as a space of exchange and participation wherever processes of hybridization occur and where it is still possible for cultures to be produced and performed without necessary mediation from the center" (p. 5).

In my view, we can incorporate the notion of borderlands as real and symbolic spaces that confine marginalized peoples in a metropolis, and the formal and informal economy. It is also helpful to integrate Esteva and Madhu's (1998) concept of the "One-Third World" and "Two-Thirds World" to address issues of geographical location and power and privilege. They proposed the categories of One-Third World and Two-Thirds World to refer to the social majorities and social minorities can be geographically located in the Global South or the Global North, and their quality of life. These categories help us understand the distribution of wealth within a history of colonization embedded in the North-South relationships. Let us look at some examples of people's lives and borderlands.

Catalina's family was partly from Puerto Rico and partly from the mainland, and her family moved back and forth from one to the other. They settled in a Latino neighborhood of a large Midwestern city where she recounted feeling not Latina enough because she was not born in Puerto Rico. Her skin tone wasn't dark enough, and she did not attend the neighborhood school that her Puerto Rican peers attended. In the gay community she was not gay enough because she considered herself bisexual. Her parents and extended family were Christian and, although she described them as somewhat religious, they did not approve of her sexual orientation. When there were conflicts with her mother, she would call Catalina "pata," a derogatory word for lesbian. Catalina knew this meant something dirty, weird, and unacceptable. She felt like there was a hole in her heart and, from a very young age, could not let go of feeling that being gay was wrong in God's eyes.

Catalina struggled with lack of acceptance outside and inside her home. She was lucky to have her aunt Martha around. Aunt Martha was the oldest of her mother's sisters and a kind of matriarch. Although she never affirmed Catalina's identity, she would chastise her sister and other family members for criticizing Catalina and remind them that family was first regardless of anybody's ways and deeds. Catalina's father kept his distance from her and her siblings. She felt his silence as disapproval but he never argued or became vindictive with her. The most intimate conversation they had occurred when Catalina was nineteen years old and already attending a local college. There was a family reunion and he had drunk too much. He told her, "I don't know what to say, *mi'ja*. I think God put a man and woman on earth to be together but I love you no matter what."

Catalina grew up witnessing and experiencing occasional racial discrimination and hearing her family's anger resulting from police harassment, store personnel racist behavior, and job managers' harshness at work. At the same time, she was told to quiet down in restaurants if she became too excited "because people here (America) do not talk in this way," and that it would be best for her children if she married a White male.

Outside her family, Catalina struggled to connect with other Latinos and everyone else, as her school was a reflection of a larger community segregated by race. African Americans, Latinos, and Whites lived in the spaces mapped by their race membership. She made friends here and there with people from each group. However, she and her sister were called "little immigrants," and both Whites and African Americans told them that they sailed to the mainland in a "cheerio." Catalina remained silent or laughed along with her classmates, as trying to fit in was less painful than fighting back. When she told her parents about these comments, they told her not to take them seriously. Catalina had to learn to develop bridges between her family and the world outside, as well as between racial groups, genders, and sexual orientations, to piece together spaces where she could be connected to all these different people and experiences that were meaningful to her. [1]

Pepe, a heterosexual, lower-middle-class and Mestizo-looking Peruvian chemist who migrated to Argentina in the wave of the 1990s, found himself working as a street peddler before he got a job as a technician in the chemical sector. He left his country in search of a better job and found himself being harshly discriminated against by Peruvian immigrants who had migrated earlier and by Argentinians. Apparently, he did not have the "right" color and did not belong to the "right" social class.

He met Rosalinda in Buenos Aires and felt they were a good match because of their similar backgrounds. Like many Peruvian women, Rosalinda worked as a maid. After three years in his job, Pepe was laid off when the company was sold, and he had to take a job with lesser pay in the textile industry. Pepe and Rosalinda lived in an immigrant-populated neighborhood and had to negotiate their survival with immigrants from Bolivia and Paraguay. This involved connecting with them around experiences of immigration and common cultural legacies while resisting racial prejudice from them and the larger Argentinian population.

Catalina, Pepe, and Rosalinda lived in a social context that forced them to negotiate boundaries and create bridges to connect and develop well-being rather than mere survival. Though I have described their contemporary circumstances, they also stand on a foundation embedded in a history of colonization and legacies of oppression from their own homelands. It is as if they carry the legacy of colonization on their backs and as if they unknowingly resist the legacy of the coloniality of being and find those in-between spaces in which to be and to create a living.

From the vantage point of the scholars in the modernity/coloniality group, border thinking arises from the colonial difference; that is, the wound of coloniality generates the formation of this kind of subjectivity. It emerges from the conflictive dialogue that decolonial thinking develops between Eurocentric thought and other languages, logics, and ways of being. For Mignolo (2000c, 2011), border thinking allows us—once having recognized inequality and accepted the wound inflicted by the colonial difference—to draw different paths and to enunciate other knowledges.

While teaching at San Diego State University, I supervised students in practica, and usually my classes were a magnet for Spanish speakers from Latin America, Chicanos, Latin@s, and anyone connected to the border. While working with them on examining dimensions of privilege around ethnicity and class in their countries of origin, I included discussions about the history of the unearned privileges we held as a result of the genocide of Indigenous populations since the arrival of Columbus in Abya Yala. I asked them to examine alternatives for taking responsibility for these unearned privileges and to explore implications in their clinical work and in their development of the self of the therapist.

One of these clinicians was a recent upper-middle-class immigrant who came from the interior of México. Her rich ethnic background involved Asian and Spanish ancestry, and she experienced great difficulty relating to the history of oppression toward Indigenous and Mestizo people in her country, or facing her position of structural privilege. Another supervisee lived in Tijuana, the city that borders San Diego. Like her peer, she was also ethnically privileged but middle rather than upper class.

The woman who cleaned and cooked for her family was an Indigenous person from the south of México. This supervisee spoke of how, after struggling with the English language and way of life, as well as discrimination, in the United States, she realized that this Indigenous woman, whose ethnicity, class, and migration struggles had been invisible to her, had possibly experienced the same, perhaps even more intense, challenges. From that point on, the supervision relationship changed. The supervisee, who initially refused to even consider the structural power that benefited her in her own society, became more willing to open up—to be humble and vulnerable in training. We were able to identify and examine the layers of power and privilege embedded in different geographical locations and we used it as a basis for working on the development of the self of the therapist (Hernández & McDowell, 2010).

COATLICUE, NEPANTLA, AND MESTIZA CONSCIOUSNESS

In the borderlands, oppressed subjectivity comprises two states: intimate terrorism or internalized oppression, and Coatlicue.[2] The latter is a state of creation. Anzaldúa (2000) called Coatlicue the process that forces us to see and confront the social constructions that have been used to represent us, usually in a pejorative manner. Coatlicue requires the strength to challenge and liberate oneself from the identities that were implanted in us through colonial discourse. This is no easy task. It is as if we are caught in between two seemingly harmful worlds. We fashion the self as the self-in-between, recognizing that the possibility of resistance lies in the creation of a new identity in the borders. This journey is characterized by the development of a critical consciousness, which Anzaldúa called Mestiza consciousness, and is akin to Freire's concept of concientización (Freire, 1971).

In *Interviews/Entrevistas* (2000), Anzaldúa explained that she began to use the term *nepantla* to expand the meaning of her original concept of borderlands:

> With the Nepantla paradigm I try to theorize unarticulated dimensions of the experience of Mestizas living in between overlapping and layered spaces of different cultures and social and geographic locations, of events and realities— psychological, sociological, political, spiritual, historical, creative, imagined. (p. 176)

Keating (2006) explained that nepantla is a Nahuatl word meaning "in-between space," and involves transformation and "dis-identification" from existing beliefs, social structures, and models of identity; by so doing, we are able to transform these existing conditions (p. 9). Nepantla is a liminal space where transformation can occur.

In the 1990s, Indian scholar Homi Bhabha (1994) contributed to the development of border thinking with his theory of the "third space." He explained:

> The possibilities of being somehow, *in between*, of occupying an interstitial space, that was not fully governed by the recognizable traditions . . . often produces a *third space*. . . It opens up a space that is skeptical of cultural totalization, of notions of identity which depend for their authority on being "ordinary" . . . a cultural identification which subverted authority. (p. 190)

It is in the interstices or spaces of articulation of cultural difference (where different cultures overlap/displace) where identities are produced, displaced, and negotiated. The concepts of nepantla and third space seem to refer to similar conditions, processes, and possibilities. Bhabha (1994) asserted an in-between third space of enunciation that is characterized by ambiguity, ambivalence, and contradictions. He described it as a space "teeming with potential" (p. 54), challenging myths of purity that define colonizing ideologies. Hybridity becomes a productive space of enunciation that opens up sites of resistance. Let's look at some concrete illustrations.

Two African American females, Nicole (age 17) and Debbie (age 18), met through the Internet. Debbie identified as lesbian and was always open about it with Nicole. Nicole thought of herself as heterosexual but was attracted to Debbie. They met and began dating. Nicole's mother opposed this relationship based on her own homophobia and accused Debbie of luring her daughter into homosexuality. Unbeknownst to Nicole, her mother involved the police by accusing Debbie of sexual involvement with a minor. Debbie was picked up by surprise and treated harshly by the local White policemen. Michelle, a Mestiza-conscious and queer activist, got involved and organized legal and community help for Debbie.

After months of dealing with the legal system, Nicole turned 18 and Debbie was able to survive the ordeal with minimal legal consequences. Michelle, Nicole, and Debbie decided to further organize to open spaces and give voice to queer youth of Color even though Nicole did not claim a specific identity based on her sexual orientation. In one of the spaces they created, other youth of Color were able to connect, and heterosexuals of Color became both learners and allies. They received affirmation from communities of people who cared about them personally and about the impact of their experience in society. They asserted their existence and challenged homophobic familial relationships as well as a racist and homophobic police and judicial system that, fortunately, failed to vilify Debbie (Maher, 2011).

In a different kind of space, my friend, colleague, and former student Pressley Ranking and I (Hernández & Rankin, 2008) examined how we created a liberatory training and therapy space addressing intersections of race, gender identity, sexual orientation, and class. At the time, I was supervising his work as a therapist in training with a same-sex affectional female couple from nationalities different than ours. Pressley and I are about the same age, but at the time I was his professor in a practicum class in a marriage and family therapy master's program. Our social locations were very different, and yet we had a lot in common. He is a male of European descent, and I am Latina, heterosexual, and an immigrant. We are both a part of a struggling middle class and fully able-bodied.

The couple was initially seen by another student in another practicum class, and their issues were framed as a "roommate situation." When Pressley expressed his opinion, initially he was subtly shut down by his supervisor and peers until they could not tolerate his insistence that this was an intimate and lesbian relationship issue. One of his peers told him that he was gay, and therefore thought everyone else was, and that he saw the world through a gay lens only.

In our supervision and training space, we explored Pressley's clinical hypotheses and supported his work. It turned out that the couple had a long and complicated intimate history, but they did not want to identify themselves as lesbian or use any kind of label. This did not deter us from assisting them to accomplish their goals for enhancing their relationship. We created a context in which our clients were validated and helped while we learned and further articulated key issues in training in the family therapy field. What did Pressley and I share? Once our intersectionalities were explored, our areas of privilege and marginalization became visible. We located ourselves in a hybrid space, nepantla, to develop a way of working that blended our knowledges and experiences and resisted silencing the voices of clients and therapist. Nepantla was a place of curiosity, risk, negotiation of meaning, and consensus on how to work with this couple.

What kind of language and human activities would constitute healing from the standpoint of nepantla? Let us look to Anzaldúa's Mestiza consciousness concept for guidance. According to Anzaldúa (1987), the process by which Mestiza consciousness, or consciousness about hybridity, is developed involves a journey whereby the person who is developing this kind of consciousness experiences a confrontation with multiple ways of knowing, which may challenge or coexist with the ones with which she is familiar (nepantla); a dismantling of identities acquired within a colonial mindset (Coatlicue); and a reconstructing of a different sense of who this person is (Coyolxauhqui). In this journey, the person realizes what she/he has to do to fit in, to be accepted, recognized, and allowed access to opportunities, rights, and resources. She/he spends time trying to be less like those considered different (lacking), and more like those who define the rules for the rest. I add that she/he also recognizes power differentials that shed light on how theories and practices that deal with cultural differences are more about colonial differences, which are named and articulated within a Eurocentric framework.

The Mestiza recognizes the struggles involved in acknowledging the various legacies that she/he embodies; she/he cannot claim a single self and so embraces multiplicity as part of her/his own identity. The Mestiza consciousness is based on the cross-pollination of experience and knowledge. There are steps for the Mestiza as she/he begins her/his life of action. These involve "taking inventory," or examining who she/he is and differentiating what she/he has learned, where, when, and from whom. After scrutinizing history and identifying lies, she/he "communicates the rupture" with oppressive traditions, "documents the struggle," "reinterprets history," and finally, "using new symbols, shapes new myths" (Anzaldúa, 1987, p. 104). This new consciousness involves expansion and inclusion of similar hybrid figures. Just as in W. E. B. DuBois's concept of "double consciousness" (1982), any refiguring of the Mestiza needs to flexibly accommodate blends of hybridities to create communities of resistance.

Anzaldúa offered many insights into the development of Mestiza consciousness in her children's book, *Prietita and the Ghost Woman* (1996), in which she explained the journey of healing the open wounds created by capitalism, nationalism, imperialism, sexism, homophobia, and racism. Prietita, a dark young girl apprenticed to a curandera (traditional healer), learns that her mother is suffering from a recurring illness. The girl, who knows that curandera Doña Lola can cure almost any illness and knows almost every healing plant, asks her for a remedio, or remedy. Doña Lola says that she has run out of ruda, a crucial ingredient in the medicine she will prepare for the mother.

Prietita then embarks in a journey to get ruda. This journey involves going to a dangerous ranch whose occupants are famous for shooting trespassers (sound familiar?).[3] Prietita does not know that, throughout the story, the figure in need of reclamation and transfiguration is La Llorona, an infamous weeping woman whose stories are known in Mexican and other Latin American cultures. In this journey, Prietita learns to listen and to trust her intuition through her experiences with various animals such as a dove, a jaguar, and a salamander. These animals can be seen as naguals, or manifestations of La Llorona, through shape shifting.

Prietita meets La Llorona above the waters of a lagoon where she is shown where to find the ruda. La Llorona leads her back to the barbed wire boundary of the ranch. Thus, La Llorona leads Prietita into a path of becoming a curandera. According to Hartley (2010), this story is symbolic of two forms of healing: the healing of the self and of the cultural status of women represented by La Llorona. He further explained that the story is a symbol for the need to develop fearless confrontation with colonialist violence, and to highlight the transmission of sacred knowledge from one generation to the next to ensure health and cultural survival.

MESTIZA CONSCIOUSNESS JOURNEYS

One of my most important life journeys to develop critical consciousness has involved addressing my own heterosexism and misuse of heterosexual privilege. Having been raised in a conservative middle-class environment where sexual orientation was as invisible as it could be, I had no idea about virtually anything related to the development, lives, dreams, and challenges of sexual minorities. My head was also filled with all sorts of garbage about sexual orientation and gender identities, but I never had to examine it. All I had before I came to the United States was one very formative experience, which, looking back, I see was the guiding force in my quest.

My maternal uncle, whom I adored and who was the most important male figure in my life, was gay. It was a family secret. I intuitively knew he was gay. No one ever told me anything about his sexual orientation, but I knew well enough to protest and argue on the few occasions when subtle derogatory comments emerged in the family. At the time, I could not and would not examine my own heterosexism. I was afraid, and all I cared about was how much I loved him. I did not quite see how my not interrogating my own homophobia was intrinsically linked to his survival.

When I came to the United States for graduate school, I was blessed to have landed in a very liberal and queer-affirming part of the country. This part of my migration experience is one of many that I am very grateful for. While living in Amherst and Northampton, Massachusetts, I had the opportunity to learn and connect with many gay, lesbian, and bisexual students and faculty. I welcomed the possibilities with open arms, knowing that I owed this to my uncle. I had to confront my own prejudices and ignorance; I had to face an ugly side of my family and, after many arguments with them, this is not a topic of conversation they engage in with me. I also lost friends, but I was not interested in making excuses or turning a blind eye to issues concerning sexual minorities. Over time I learned about how to move beyond my interpersonal life to advocate and resist heteronormative systems and homophobic institutions.

I embarked on a journey to examine my own gender identity development and sexual orientation, thanks to my uncle and the Amherst/Northampton community that embraced me in spite of my ignorance. This journey has not ended, for even if I think that I am not personally heterosexist, I am marked by the privilege of my social location as a heterosexual, and this connects me and impacts my relations with heterosexuals and gays, lesbians, bisexuals, transgenders, and others alike.

INTERSECTING IDENTITIES

Identities constructed on the basis of gender, ethnicity, class, ability, and sexual orientation are socially significant, and context-specific ideological constructs are useful as markers for historical and social location (Martín-Alcoff, Hames-García, Mohanty, & Moya, 2006). These identities are especially relevant when considering how they intersect in a particular social context, thereby making visible the structural privileges (i.e., access, opportunity, and opinion), or lack thereof, that people have simply by virtue of their location (e.g., lesbian, lower-class, fully able-bodied women of Color; or heterosexual, upper-middle-class, visually impaired women of Color). Collins (1998) explained that looking at intersecting identities "highlights how social groups are positioned within unjust power relations, but it does so in a way that introduces added complexity to formerly race-, class-, and gender-only approaches to social phenomena" (p. 205).

The concept of intersecting identities offers an interpretive framework to analyze the ways in which a group's privileges and marginalization affect each other. The concept can potentially become a resource for social change. For example, if we look at differences in sexual orientation, ability, and class among Latin@s, we see that increased potentials for safety, life, business partnerships, and employment accrue to those who happen to be heterosexual, able-bodied, and upper-middle-class. Their experiences in the United States and in their own countries of origin must be understood within the context of these intersections to address issues of privilege and accountability in a manner that does justice to their complex intersectional identities. Let us look at some examples.

Liliana and Marcela are both family therapists. Liliana's family migrated from Guatemala to the United States and worked as day laborers until they saved enough to open their own small business. She is lesbian, dark, able-bodied, and college-educated and has kept herself in the middle class in spite of the amount she owes in educational loans. While she was the first one in her family to attend college, and has accomplished much due to her pioneer spirit and tenacity, she never learned how to relate to people from higher social classes or to middle-class people of European descent. She is shy and apprehensive because of the many experiences of discrimination that she and her family have had.

Contrast the opportunities and access that Marcela, a heterosexual, able-bodied daughter of immigrants from Venezuela, has had. She was born into a family with college-educated wealthy parents. Her family migrated from a town in Cataluña, Spain, to Venezuela, and her last name is not overly common. She speaks three languages and has traveled extensively in Europe and Asia. Her social graces are outstanding, and her ability to generate professional connections has helped her gain visibility in desirable professional spaces. Marcela's social location affords her access and opportunity that Liliana does not have. This does not mean that Liliana is completely disadvantaged or that she may not get a job for which both apply, but it helps us understand how putting these two women under the category of Latina or Hispanic obscures crucial differences between them. Let's look at another example.

One fateful December 31st night, my husband and I decided to take both of our cars to Annapolis, Maryland, to celebrate New Year's at a restaurant. All of our friends were Latin@s. He traveled with Juan, an old friend of mine, who we did not know was undocumented at the time. I traveled with a friend who was finishing up her doctorate, and her children. I was stopped by the police for driving 35 mph in a 25 mph zone. I failed to notice the sign, which was my fault, and I wouldn't have challenged getting a ticket.

However, before I had a chance to hear about a ticket, the policemen asked me to get out of the car, searched me, and handcuffed me without an explanation. Three heavily armed men surrounded me in spite of my obeying their orders and posing no threat. They took me into the back of their car, and when I kept asking what the reason for their actions was and requested that they check my social security number, they told me that I had the right to a call once I was booked in jail. In the meantime, my friend protested their actions and quickly called my husband, a White heterosexual college-educated male, and told him what was happening. The police witnessed the conversation and, after his initial refusal, one of the policemen finally told her the address of the police station where I was detained.

Although I had made risky decisions in the past while doing human rights work in Colombia and had felt fear for my life, these circumstances could not compare to experiencing the impact of White supremacy in my own body. Next, they put me in a jail cell and locked the door while I was still in handcuffs. I still did not know the reason for these actions. I knew to stay calm and continue to be respectful to try to avoid further abuse, but inside I was praying for help. After one of the officers came to ask me if I knew any English (keep in mind that they had my wallet with my driver's license and university ID, and I had been talking to them all this time in English), we continued to converse in English as he asked me where I was from, what I did for a living, etc. Then they took me out of the cell, took the handcuffs off, and sat me in a chair where I heard their opinions about immigrants and especially "Hispanics." They went on to tell me that I had not explained to them who I was.

In the meantime, my husband arrived and demanded an explanation while arguing with them. I was taken out, my wallet was returned, and my husband had another argument with the officer who led this process. We got no apologies. He explained that there was a woman in the system with my first name and one of my last names, Maria Hernández, and that she was sought for dealing drugs. I wondered if these men had the most minimal clue. Did they know how many women with the name "Maria Hernández" have migrated to or were born in this country?

In spite of the humiliation and horror of this experience, being fully fluent, having documents, a university ID, a bilingual friend who advocated for me, and a White husband who raised hell in the station, are concrete expressions of the social capital that I have by virtue of my education, class, and marriage. This was an experience of victimization, yet the justice system never even considered it an issue worth pursuing. There was no justice. However, my social location still made it possible for me to survive the ordeal with less harm than that experienced by others. Do you know how powerful White privilege is? Well, our friend Juan drove with my husband to the station and even walked inside with him. He was the most at risk because he had no documents at the time, but no one ever asked him a question.

Others may be familiar with a common scenario in the United States, exemplified by a mental health professional and scholar that I will call Martín. Martín identifies as Latino but makes sure who everyone knows that he is European by way of family ancestry, travel and customs, and education and professional and family networks. Typically, such individuals move up in the career ladder by empathizing with the Latino cause when it is convenient for them (e.g., affirmative action), but their most intimate circles are other Latinos like them and those of European descent. It is as if they have a code by which they signal that they are not really one of "them," and that they are willing to use this group of people for their own benefit and that of the system.

Consider an immigrant, college-educated psychologist (or mental health professional) from the Southern Cone who built up his career based on working with Latinos. Let's say that a central aspect of his research agenda and past clinical practice was working with Mexican immigrants, Mexican Americans, Puerto Ricans, Dominicans, and second- and third-generation Latinos from disempowered communities. However, he grew up in an upper-middle-class home and had all the privileges that a White male has in his country of origin. He suffers the pain of racialization in the United States where he, like all of us, discovers that "he has a race," and becomes part of an ethnic minority group; he experiences discrimination due to his accent and olive skin color.

He cries about the loss of privilege he suffered in the United States, but discovers that he is really not like "them." He is educated, well-mannered, charming, and has more in common with any middle-class American of European descent than with a Latino from the ghetto. He finds a way to navigate the system to get the most benefit, in this case by using the people-of-Color agenda when he stands to benefit and by making sure that he differentiates himself from "them," showing his European credentials and those of his country. In the meantime he reveals a ferocious competition against any other Latin American and/or Latino immigrants or colleagues of Color who might question his location and tactics. Sound familiar? In the meantime he uses his popularity among mostly heterosexual women of European descent to be recommended as a consultant, speaker, and expert in immigration matters.

Another familiar scenario from my own country involves an assessment of class credentials by which people easily locate where you belong in the social hierarchy by asking what neighborhood you were raised in or what neighborhood your family lives in and where you went to school. With this minimal information people from upper-middle- and upper-class backgrounds can quickly decide to move forward with a conversation and, if doing so, what kind of relationship they will establish and what information they will share about themselves.

Let's take a similar scenario in another geographical space. In Colombia, few families inherited the wealth of stolen lands and slavery throughout the country. Many of the Criollo families who pride themselves on their European ancestry show their credentials via their last names and/or family trees in addition to property, education, connections, etc. Many of these families have had a very close connection with the Catholic Church through sons who have occupied high positions in the church and can influence the country's local and national governments.

Consider the case of Alfonso, a gay man born to a family of Spanish lineage who was raised within one of the most traditional of Catholic priest organizations from elementary to graduate school. He lives a double life and can do so comfortably as a college professor and a philosopher because there are many powerful men in the same situation with families who simply choose to look the other way. He has a myriad of connections at hand due to his family's extensive social capital and his own connections through elite Catholic organizations. He competes for a department chair position with Claudia, a heterosexual female who has no connections to the church and a family who struggled to put her through college. She advanced due to merit and studied abroad. She is divorced and has a child, and her husband does not pay child support. Like most in this social context, she has little or no awareness about her own heterosexism. The nuances of social locations, the differences that social capital makes, and the complexities of systems of power must all be examined.

Bourdeiu (1986) defined social capital as "the aggregate of the actual or potential resources which are linked to possession of a durable network of more or less institutionalized relationships of mutual acquaintance or recognition" (p. 248) and as a capital made up of connections that affirm bonds of friendships, status, recognition and have the potential to become economic capital. Let's unpack Alfonso's situation in the previous example in light of this definition. He creates social situations (e.g., dinners, going to movies) that he knows are key to the development of professional relationships. He also shares his tastes, desires, and knowledge of food, travels, people, clothing, etc., with colleagues and potential partners in project ventures. Thus, when it comes to "representing" Latinos in venues that are worth competing for (e.g., grants, conference presentations, and leadership positions), he is thought of highly and considered before anyone who may seem a "troublemaker" or simply someone who does not fit as well. At this point he does not have to work so hard to get what he needs. He is in.

If we look at Alfonso and Claudia's situations, we can hypothesize that, by virtue of his inherited status, social networks, and wealth, no matter how bright she is, it is likely that in the patriarchal context of a religious university system embedded in the traditional and very patriarchal values of a city such as Bogotá, Claudia has little chance of getting the chair position. However, Alfonso lives with the pain of marginalization and internalized oppression in a larger social context that rejects his sexual orientation. He also had to learn to be cautious and careful to protect his personal safety in highly heterosexist environments.

INTERSECTIONALITY

Mohanty (2003) affirmed that the concept of intersectionality helps us unveil power relationships not reducible to binary oppositions between oppressor and oppressed by attending to fluid and multiple "structures of domination that intersect to locate women differently at particular historical conjunctures, while insisting on the dynamic oppositional agency of individuals and collectives and their engagement in 'daily life'" (p. 55). She clarified that systems of racial, class, and gender domination do not have identical effects on everyone everywhere. Privilege and marginalization affect access and opportunity of entire groups, families, and individuals. Individual experience and interpretation of privilege and marginalization will vary with each person, but individual frames of reference are not the yardstick to measure larger social issues that affect us all in one way or another at various times.

In the mental health fields, Prilleltensky and Prilleltensky (2006), Hernández, Almeida, and Dolan Del-Vecchio (2005), and, in cultural studies, Escobar (2008) have concurred that cultural differences are not the source of power differentials and they should not be the framework on which mental health services are designed. Instead, differences in power associated with particular cultural meanings and practices generate norms and meaning-making practices that define what is dominant and marginal, accepted or not, in the worlds of everyday social life and mental health training and practice. An intersectionality framework should be used along with nepantla because it allows us to see how dimensions of privilege and marginalization vary in context, and how one has to look at all dimensions and their impact on the self and others in a fluid manner.

"WE DON'T HAVE THESE PROBLEMS HERE; THESE PROBLEMS OCCUR IN THE UNITED STATES, NOT HERE."

How often have you heard in Latin American countries that racism does not exist there? How often have you heard that there is 100 percent gender equality? Isn't it all about class differences? The Latin American left and the legacies of leftist European thinking linger in the social consciousness, the social disciplines, and important niches of innovation and concern for social justice in Latin American circles. Here is an example of a somewhat common argument about why colonization and decolonization are not parameters fitting all contexts in Latin America.

In a presentation where I discussed some ideas about decolonization and psychology training along the lines of what I had discussed so far at the Interamerican Psychology Congress, an Argentinian psychology student stated that, although these ideas were interesting, they did not really apply to

Argentina because, in contrast with the U.S. colonization process, colonization was not essential to how capitalism was implemented in his country, and in fact, the social sciences did not go through a process of systematization like in the United States. In his view, this fact allowed psychoanalysts to monopolize the production of knowledge and the practice of mental health for a long time, and this deterred the mental health field from developing strong liaisons between psychology and the market as had happened in the United States. In addition, soviet psychology also had a strong legacy there and this psychology is not capitalist. And finally, he affirmed that his country had no legacy of colonization because there are no ethnic minorities there, no people of African descent, only peoples with different nationalities.

I was thankful for his comment as it allowed me to discuss with more depth how psychoanalysis and soviet psychology are other forms of Eurocentered thinking, and how if we keep thinking that there are only two options that must live in opposition, that is, capitalism and socialism, we will continue Cold-War-era dualistic thinking with limited horizons for change. Let's highlight some common prevailing ideas that his comment reflected: (a) the frame of reference is between the United States and Europe; (b) psychoanalysis and soviet psychology are seen as the alternatives—but these systems of knowledge were produced using European languages and reproduced by European immigrants in Abya Yala; in other words, what is framed as an alternative is more of the same; (c) Indigenous peoples, sexual minorities, and other marginalized populations are invisible (would they have visibility as objects of study?); (d) there is no memory of the history of genocide that African and Indigenous peoples experienced in the Southern Cone and the legacies of privilege that the psychology student embodies; and (e) differences are categorized by nationality because Argentina is a country with a long history of European and Latin American migration. But guess who tends to be dark and who tends to be light? And guess what nationalities have more status? Furthermore, the speaker did not explicitly address his own social and epistemic location, which in this case, makes various dimensions of privilege invisible.

Grosfoguel (2006), in line with Fannon (1967), affirmed that the success of coloniality has been to produce people who think like oppressors even though their social location and life conditions are those of marginalization. In his view the Latin American elites who live in Latin America live and think like colonizers, and many ethnic minority populations in the United States are colonized subjects who think from a decolonial perspective. This view helps us reaffirm the importance of using the concepts of nepantla, intersectionality, Global South and Global North, and One-Third/Two-Thirds Worlds together.

SOCIAL LOCATION AND EPISTEMIC LOCATION

An intersecionality analysis must also include a distinction between social location and epistemic location. Grosfoguel (2007, 2008a, 2008b), Lugones (2007), and Mignolo (2011) have explained that a person or group can be located on dominant sides of the intersectionality matrix (e.g., gender, class, race, sexual orientation, ability) and take an epistemic position consistent with the marginalized position in a power relationship. Likewise, people whose social locations are that of marginalization may take oppressive epistemic positions.

For example, in a study exploring how marriage, couple, and family therapist-educators with privileged social locations position themselves to make a difference in larger social systems, McDowell and I (2012) found that participants recognized that the relationship between privilege and lack of privilege has to do with class and ethnicity and that those who have social privileges stand on and benefit from those who do not have those privileges. An illustration of this idea follows:

> If I can afford to live in a nice house in the suburbs . . . in a society where there's differential pay, the only way I can afford it is if someone else can't. And if the person who comes to clean earned as much as I do then we couldn't pay her to clean which means we're maintaining that difference. . . . Even though my parents didn't have much money, I strongly believe because I had access to state universities and I'm White, I could over time earn more. . . . So those disparities start early and get bigger and bigger. (p. 169)

One response to becoming aware of the relationship between privilege and lack of privilege is to shift from focusing on the oppression and lack of privilege of others to dismantling the privilege from which one benefits. We continued our analysis by pointing out that, over time, participants started to try to change the very structures that benefited them and not others, for example:

> Initially . . . my belief system was more liberal. . . . I didn't make the connection [that because] I have education . . . [and] access to power, then it's my, I would have never of said obligation, it's my desire to work on behalf of people who don't have what I have, so in that sense, I think I had that kind of liberal belief that with privilege comes responsibility. I think what changed was getting increasingly aware that the very things that protected and advanced my privilege were things that were withheld or barriers to other people. And so it was like this shift to instead of using my privilege to work for them . . . how do I use my privilege to dismantle the [systems of] privilege that I'm a part of? . . . It took some time to learn that just being caring and wanting things to be different for people who are the target of oppression is not the same as tackling the systems and individuals responsible for the oppression. (p. 169)

Persons or groups whose social locations may be that of marginalization and who take oppressive epistemic positions include conservative Christian, African American, and Latino churches that condemn any form of marital arrangement other than a heterosexual, religiously sanctioned partnership; ethnic minority groups or persons who support the persecution of undocumented Latin@s in the United States; and women of Color who compete with other women of Color and use the same oppressive strategies that are typically used against them. Let's look at the following example in more detail.

Carlos, a Latino, gay, fully able-bodied faculty member at a university with no tenure system, came to therapy searching for a safe place to talk about his difficulties at work. He had been working at a university for four years, and although his publication record was competitive, his student evaluations ranged between good and excellent, and his administrative duties were fulfilled, he kept having trouble after trouble with the program's administrative assistant, a White heterosexual woman in her forties, and the African American heterosexual program director after he opposed hiring a conservative religious African American woman into the program. In fact, in the past, when he complained about a guest male faculty in the closet pressuring him to date, his colleagues cast doubt on his complaints and dismissed them. The program director, his administrative assistant, and the cleaning crew, who also happened to be African American, kept complaining about his facial expressions, tone of voice, and general communication so that he almost stopped talking to anyone in the office for fear of being misinterpreted. The program director complained to Human Resources by stating that he "was intimidating," "intense," and "angry." This man used the same old tactics that have been used against his people to force his colleague out. Carlos had developed a stomach ulcer by the time he began therapy. Therapy helped him process his thinking and face his sadness and anger, but ultimately he had to find another job.

In sum, social location and epistemic location differ depending on the kind of choices we make relative to how we use our own privilege and marginalization and how we position ourselves in our family, organizational, and community systems. Sometimes social and epistemic locations coincide, and sometimes they do not. However, thinking of oneself as someone who questions and challenges privilege at any level is not an excuse to make invisible one's privilege.

In addition to differentiating social location from epistemic location, it is necessary to distinguish between identity politics and identity in politics. A critique has been made about the risks of intolerance and fundamentalism involved in assuming that identities are essential aspects of individuals (Martín-Alcoff, Hames-García, Mohanty, & Moya, 2006). Unfortunately, some of the writings in multicultural psychology, multicultural counseling, and multicultural family therapy (Lum, 2007) have contributed to the essentialization of ethnicity, gender, and sexual orientation by generating counseling models for specific ethnic groups as if all Latinos share the same foundational characteristics. This has led, for example, to ideas about how all Latinos value family, have a present-centered time orientation, and other assumptions that cannot apply to all Latinos in the United States. Thus, the practice of essentializing difference in multicultural scholarship results in otherizing (Almeida, Hernández-Wolfe, and Tubbs, 2011).

Freire (1971), Anzaldúa (1987, 2000), and hooks (1992) used the concept of *other* to describe the acts of naming, categorizing, and classifying as acts of power used to demarcate the center from the periphery, the normal from the abnormal, the same from the different, and self from other. An alternative path to addressing identity and politics involves looking at identity in politics. Mignolo (2007) argued for the relevance of identity in politics because the control of identity politics lies precisely in the construction of an identity that doesn't look as such but as the "natural" appearance of the world. That is, Whiteness, heterosexuality, and manhood are the main features of an identity politics that denounces similar but opposing identities as something that is considered essential and fundamental. However, the dominant identity politics doesn't manifest itself as such, but through abstract universals such as science, philosophy, Christianity, liberalism, Marxism, and the like (pp. 43-72).

Therefore, resistance that highlights marginalized identities has a place in our lives, not because we are all Latin@s, women, or sexual minorities, but because we resist within a way of understanding the world and living as a community. From a nepantla perspective, resistance accompanies all forms of domination and lives in the fissures and silences of hegemonic narratives, in the practices of remembering involving our oral and written traditions, and in our very bodies and ways of relating.

LOS ENCUENTROS DE VOCES (GATHERING OF VOICES): A NEPANTLA SPACE

The emergence and development of this nepantla space illustrates the challenges that Western psychology and mental health in general encounter in the Global South and in working with people located in the Two-Thirds. It shows the tensions between compartmentalized areas of practice in psychology (e.g., clinical vs. community) and the power differentials that set the stage for colonizing practices that intend to help but perhaps don't.

In her work with displaced populations and people living in poverty around the outskirts of southern Bogotá, Carolina Nensthiel (2012) described some of the challenges that she faced in trying to provide therapeutic services to women experiencing domestic violence in this needy community. She was hired by the local government to implement a plan that sought to respond to domestic violence by offering individual therapy. A space was opened to provide services in the headquarters shared with many other community development projects. However, these services had a peculiar characteristic: women in the community did not request them. Therefore, some women from the community were hired to reach out to other women, acting as peer educators based on their training in issues of domestic violence.

Nensthiel led the implementation of this service. She and her team found themselves listening, in the privacy of individual therapy sessions, to stories that were all very similar in that they encompassed the effects of multiple needs and oppressions related to poverty, isolation, and disconnection. After reflecting on the commonality of issues and the challenges of getting women to come to therapy on a regular basis, Nensthiel began to hold group therapy sessions in which she opened the conversational space to the peer educators and invited them to share their perspectives with everyone else. Through this process, everyone began to learn to compassionately listen to each other, and, with time, the women in the community sought their peer educators to talk about their problems.

Nensthiel observed how these webs of understanding and trust developed, and she worked with the peer educators to develop a witnessing and listening stance as they continued their involvement with women in the community. At the time she thought that their role was more appropriately described as that of someone who listens, and she called them "women listeners," or "mujeres escucha." As the groups continued, women in the community were more interested in attending group gatherings with the mujeres escucha than individual therapy. This led to a change in the position and role of the therapists. Therapists shared the facilitation of gatherings with the mujeres escucha, and the therapists' stance of expertise, distance, and lack of self-disclosure became more permeable. The therapists, the "mujeres escucha," and the women shared their reflections in open conversational spaces. Therapists were asked to be careful to avoid making their comments the center of conversations, but they were free to reflect on the impact that the women's experiences had on them. The groups became an outlet for women to connect around the shared experiences of domestic violence, but they also became a place to share their joys and to find support and kinship.

Nensthiel was later involved in an elective course for psychology students completing their last year of practical training at a private university in Bogotá. This course was part of the social and community psychology track and involved a participatory action research component. Nensthiel initiated a collaboration between this psychology program and the local government in southern Bogotá, where she worked. The project was designed to develop therapeutic services that fit the community's needs and idiosyncrasies. Using her training in family therapy and community psychology, Nensthiel began to integrate ideas from narrative approaches (e.g., definition ceremonies), collaborative approaches (e.g., reflecting teams), Alcoholics Anonymous, community psychology, and participatory action research to design a space that would change the balance of power between therapists and clients, and breach boundaries between the private and public spheres of life. She called this space for dialogue and community building "Encuentros de Voces" (gathering of voices).

The Encuentros de Voces are collective improvisational conversation spaces in which participants dialogue together and witness each other's stories. They are framed by the idea that the stories shared are gifts worthy of honor. Facilitators invite participants to move along the continuum of private and public conversation by sharing their own internal dialogues with the group. The facilitators also offer questions and reflections and prevent participants from using conversional styles or commenting in ways that may be hurtful and inappropriate. As they resonate with the stories shared, participants and therapists contribute to the dialogue by anchoring their reflections in their own personal history. This collective experience intends to challenge isolation, create webs of solidarity, and create critical awareness about gender identity, class, and race issues (Nensthiel, 2012).

Descriptive data and a qualitative analysis of data from samples of these Encuentros de Voces, as well as focus groups with community members and students in training, and murals created in the neighborhoods, showed that these gatherings contributed to the reconstruction of the social fabric in the seven locales in which they were regularly implemented. Data from participants indicate that women developed networks of friends and became involved in taking care of each other. They also developed solidarity initiatives for supporting participants when they were ill or experiencing a crisis, and became more aware of gender inequities and class prejudice as well as personal agency around relationships, family, and jobs.

Data from students in training show the positive impact of parallel processes between the Encuentros and their class relative to fostering democratic participation; learning from the context and practice of these gatherings; questioning disciplinary dichotomies (e.g., social/community vs. clinical psychology); developing critical consciousness about class, gender, race, and sexual orientation privilege; and learning to move between the private and public nature of the Encuentros.

The Encuentros de Voces were first implemented in 2008, and by mid-2011 students were holding approximately 150 gatherings per term in seven locales in the southern outskirts of Bogotá. Ironically, the gatherings were mostly attended by women because the project mandate and the politics at decision-making levels in the government restricted them to women, although a small group of men and gay, lesbian, and bisexual persons attended some of the gatherings. In spite of these and other political challenges, the Encuentros de Voces exemplify how Nensthiel, her students, and the community members who cocreated these spaces of dialogue forged a practice in between private and public, community and clinical, by transforming a mandate for services—that not only proved unsuccessful but imposed a way of healing based on Eurocentric standards that has the potential to be a practice of colonization—into a nepantla space.

SUMMARY

The coloniality of being involves the systemic suppression of local knowledges and the emergence of alternative knowledges resulting from this experience of pervasive marginalization. Nepantla is a liminal space where transformation can occur and is situated within unarticulated dimensions of experience where people live in between overlapping and layered psychological, sociological, political, spiritual, and historical spaces. These spaces are a potential fertile ground for the emergence and articulation of alternative knowledges. Developing these knowledges involves a journey of change in consciousness that can be metaphorically described as intimate terrorism, Coatlicue, Coyolxauhqui, and Mestiza consciousness. This journey must also involve an examination of intersecting identities, social location, and epistemic location to understand and articulate the ways in which gender identities, class, race, sexual orientation, and ability intersect and make visible both privilege and marginalization as well as nepantla spaces. If the reader is interested in using this material for further reflection, I provide a set of open-ended questions for dialogue in the Appendix.

NOTES

1. For a history of the colonization of Puerto Rico, see *Decolonization Models for America's Last Colony* by Ángel Collado Schwartz, and *Constructing a Colonial People: 1898–1932*, by Pedro Cabán. For a discourse analysis of social work representations of immigrants, see Park and Kemp (2006) in the journal *Social Service Review*.

2. Coatlicue, "The Mother of Gods," is the Aztec goddess who gave birth to the moon, stars, and Huitzilopochtli, the god of the sun and war. She is also known as Toci, or "our grandmother," and "the lady of the serpent," the patron of women who die in childbirth.

3. President Obama's record on immigration is dismal. During his administration, deportations have risen to a record 400,000 individuals a year, through the unparalleled expansion of immigration enforcement measures. The administration also has a record of making grand announcements about providing relief based on discretionary process. So far, these have amounted to no more than recycled memos and broken promises. See the website deportation-nation.org as well as reports from the *Los Angeles Times* and the *New York Times*. The president's partial implementation of the DREAM Act, in which he uses executive privilege just months before the November 2012 election, is a sad reflection of his government's approach to immigration and Latinos.

Chapter Four

Trauma, Resistance/Resilience, and the Colonial Difference

Something is observed or experienced by a community, and the symbols and sequences of the mythology are given together in an event that appears so much out of the ordinary experiential sequence as to impress itself upon the collective memories of the community for a sufficiently long duration of time. . . . The symbols are always representations of the concrete and the place always has precise location.

—Vine Deloria, 2003, p. 75

The connectedness of past to present to future remains a circle of lessons and insights that can give us both the consciousness and the conscience to heal ourselves. Understanding the interrelationship with our past and how it shapes our present world will also give us the courage to initiate healing.

—Maria Yellow Horse Brave Heart and Lemyra M. DeBruyn, 1998, p. 76

In chapter 2, I discussed the underpinnings of the modernity/coloniality collaborative project (Escobar, 2007) as a way to create a new musical score, so to speak, or a new horizon of meaning. Key concepts included the *coloniality of power*, which refers to a global hegemonic model of power that joins race, gender, sexual orientation, labor, and geographical spaces based on the needs of capital and in support of the welfare of White European peoples (Quijano, 2000a; Lugones, 2010); the *colonial difference* refers to the processes that create the "other" by the coloniality of power, and to an epistemic location (where we situate ourselves to create knowledge), that of a border consciousness (Mignolo, 2000a). The colonial difference highlights the relationships between cultural differences and global power structures.

In chapter 3, I examined Anzaldúa's (2000) concept of nepantla and related concepts such as intersectional identities (Martín-Alcoff, Hames-

García, Mohanty, & Moya, 2006) and identities in politics (Grosfoguel, 2012; Mignolo, 2010). These concepts helped us create a foundation for locating interpersonal problems in a larger context where intersections of privilege and marginalization shape people's interpersonal relationships as well as their relations with the land and the spirit. In this chapter, I will examine trauma, and resistance and resilience, from the standpoint of the colonial difference.

TRAUMATIC STRESS AND RESILIENCE

The research fields concerning traumatic stress and resilience have followed different trajectories and emerged within distinct social environments. However, within the academic and professional worlds of family therapy and other mental health fields, both have remained grounded in Eurocentered thinking. For example, the modern field of traumatic stress studies in the United States emerged within political and social movements such as the African American and other civil rights movements, Stonewall, women's movements, and antiwar protests. In particular, the movements during the 1960s and 1970s against the U.S. war on Vietnam, and the European and Israeli advocacy of those who experienced World War II and the Nazi holocaust led to the inclusion of post-traumatic stress disorder (PTSD) in the *Diagnostic and Statistical Manual of Mental Disorders* (Brown & APA, 2008; Herman, 1992).

Bessel van der Kolk's (1984) pioneering studies with Vietnam veterans provide evidence of the existence and persistence of trauma after exposure to war. This evidence has impacted the world of medicine through psychiatry, as well as psychology and the social and political arena, which continued to deny that exposure to war left drastic effects on the human body. In spite of this history, L. Brown (2008) commented that "it might have been reasonable to assume that these socially conscious professionals, already deeply attuned to some forms of social injustice, would have looked next to issues of racism, classism, heterosexism, and other forms of oppressive inequality as they tried to enhance their comprehension of how trauma affected human lives; but that never occurred" (p. 8).

Many Latin American academics in psychology adopted U.S. scholars' definition of trauma, critiqued the American diagnosis of PTSD, and attuned themselves to social injustice in relation to the effects of dictatorships, civil war, and community work in contexts of poverty. However, they did not systematically and comprehensively address issues of racism, heterosexism, and other forms of oppressive inequality, or the historical legacy of genocide perpetrated on Indigenous peoples and Afro-descendants. My experience in some Latin American countries is that there is a schism between "clinical" and "social/community" psychology at the levels of theory, training, and practice, which prevents an urgently needed integration of such knowledge and the development of new, cohesive, and locally grounded knowledge and practices to heal the wounds of historical and current trauma.

The trauma field in the United States has been internationalized due to the many social conflicts occurring around the globe. Many authors working outside of the United States have addressed the lack of congruence and the imposition of a trauma framework that does not account for the role of social structures and perpetrators, or of inequality, continuity, intensity, and frequency of violence in countries facing political repression or war around the globe (Becker, 1995; Beristain, 1999; Herman, 1992; Hernandez, 2002a; Summerfield, 1995; Waller, 1996). However, their critiques still fell short of addressing their own Eurocentrism.

For example, in his 1995 essay on the deficiencies of the PTSD concept, Becker pointed out that the word *post* suggests that "the traumatic event was limited to a certain event in time" (p. 101) in the past; and that labeling victims of political repression, genocide, or torture as *disordered* due to the symptoms they experience is unethical. Furthermore, he asserted that victims "expect that the system will look after them and protect them, but the system, like the offender, simply uses the victim for its own purposes" (p. 83).

Many others followed (Beristain, 1999; Summerfeld, 2004), and the field expanded to try to address the complexities of the impact of war, political persecution, and natural disasters. However, we did not address our own social positioning, our privilege, and the legacies of colonization that we stood upon as we tried to address conceptual and practical issues in working with trauma. Only very recently have some scholars engaged the political dimensions of trauma work in connection with legacies of colonization, race, and class (L. Brown, 2008; Carter, 2007; Kirmeyer, 2006, 2012a, 2012b; Henningsen & Kirmayer, 2000; Braveheart, Yellowheart, 1998, 1999a, 1999b, 2000, 2001, 2003, 2007). For example, Brown (2008) wrote the following:

> Genocide perpetrated against Europeans has been of interest in the trauma field; genocide perpetrated by Europeans against Indigenous people as colonial forces invaded the Western Hemisphere and the Global South has for the most part not been a subject of the field's attentions if one simply adds up the number of publications and conference presentations. The descendants and beneficiaries of the colonizers are among those controlling the professional discourse far more often than are the descendants of the colonized. (p. 10)

In Central and South Abya Yala there is wide consensus about the inadequacy of the PTSD diagnosis, but those who have made these valid and valuable critiques exhibit little to no recognition of their own position in their societies, which, for the most part, have remained socially exclusionary and openly racist. As the work on the fifth edition of the *Diagnostic and Statistical Manual of Mental Disorders* continues in the United States, advocates for the inclusion of the complex PTSD diagnosis, who have been working for decades to expand our conceptualization of traumatic stress responses, will likely see the acknowledgement of their extremely valuable efforts. However, it is also likely that the diagnosis will continue to receive worldwide critiques because of the ways in which Anglo American diagnostic nosology is an agent of globalization, imposing its highly biased constructs of health and healing under the guise of a standard and universal diagnostic system (Droždek, Wilson, & Turkovic, 2012).

The study of trauma and traumatic stress responses within a framework of colonization and decolonization requires us to look at historical and social contexts to make sense of massive and intergenerational trauma responses. For when we choose to focus solely on the present and on specific medical symptoms, we again fall into assuming that a part of the picture constitutes the whole. In addition, by focusing only on individual expressions of pain and their medicalization, we remove from the equation the systems that created this pain and the systems that continue to perpetuate it. Paying attention to how pain and healing connect interpersonally and communally is essential to bringing cooperation and restoration into the lives of everyone on the planet.

For example, in spite of the complex and challenging historical legacies of conquest, colonization, and oppression in Abya Yala resulting from the interaction of disease, collision of worldviews, and ways of living—and sometimes collaboration of indigenous groups with Europeans against other indigenous groups—it is impossible for me to be blind to the ways in which I, like many other Mestizos, have benefited from the historical expropriation of lands, racial discrimination, and lack of access and opportunities that my indigenous ancestors endured. In spite of my own family's history of political persecution (not uncommon in many Colombian families as a result of "The Violence") and the various and continued challenges that they have faced, I still had access and opportunity resulting from the privilege of my social location. Understanding this interconnectedness helps me place myself within this context to make informed decisions about how to give back, to be accountable, and to support those who struggle more than I do with marginalization.

Brave Heart (1998, 1999a, 1999b) and Brave Heart and her colleagues (2011) and other scholars (Brave Heart & DeBruyn, 1998; Campbell, Christopher, & Evans-Campbell, 2011; Duran & Duran, 1995; Duran, 2006; Gagné, 1998; Shepard, O'Neill, & Guenette, 2006; Wiechelt, Gryczynski, Johnson, & Caldwell, 2012) have articulated the ways in which historical trauma relates to current trauma for Indigenous peoples. They have also established parallels between their work and that of scholars who pioneered the idea of intergenerational trauma (Danieli, 1985, 2007) and even those who established a neurobiological basis for explaining how the interpersonal and the neurobiological aspects of human functioning connect across generations (Yehuda et al., 1998).

Brave Heart (2000, 2001, 2003, 2007) advanced a conceptualization in which historical trauma and contemporary trauma responses relate to a lifetime of, and to intergenerational experiences of, oppression. She explained that historical trauma and historical trauma responses are related to such psychological outcomes as unresolved grief, complicated/prolonged grief, PTSD, and depression, all of which are often comorbid with substance abuse. This framework helps us understand these psychological problems in context, reduce stigma, and address healing from approaches that restore well-being within a framework embedded in the traditions of communities, while attending to and incorporating relevant contemporary knowledge produced in the medical and psychological framework of the West.

Research conducted in Latin America with Indigenous peoples also points to the need to use a historical framework and to address the impact of unresolved grief, collective trauma, and behavioral health issues (Beristain, Paez, & Gonzalez, 2000; Beristain, 1999; Gone & Alcantara, 2007). For example, Sabin, Cardozo, Nackerud, Kaiser, and Varese (2003) examined how Maya communities from Guatemala and México have been found to suffer from collective and ongoing trauma and prolonged grief symptoms; Pedersen, Tremblay, Errazuriz, and Gamarra (2008) examined linkages between social context and the collective experience of forced migration and the survival of Indigenous peoples from the Peruvian highlands, arguing for the need to move beyond the notion of PTSD to address the multiple levels and kinds of suffering that result from massive historical traumatic experiences.

Another body of scholarly work addressing race-related stress, trauma, and ethnoviolence as catalysts for traumatic stress helps us understand the relationships between the pervasiveness and impact of racial oppression and health. In his 2007 review on racism and psychological and emotional injury, Carter offered a comprehensive overview of race-based stress and trauma, indicating that the heightened stress from the chronic, comprehensive, and cumulative effects of racism and perceived discrimination has been associated with decreased quality of life, negative self-esteem, intrusive thoughts, hypertension, and increased risk for mental and physical illness such as depression, anxiety, or headaches in African Americans (Clark, Anderson, Clark, & Williams, 1999; Landrine & Klonoff, 1996; Hopkins, 1993; Utsey et al., 2002; Utsey, Ponterotto, Reynolds, & Cancelli, 2000).

Carter (2007) developed and defined "race-based traumatic stress injury" (p. 88), a nonpathological constellation of emotional reactions to racism stress that is potentially similar to those that characterize PTSD, with the caveat that such reactions are the person's subjective experience of the events or incidents and not necessarily in agreement with the perception that others may have of an event as traumatic. He argued that this kind of traumatic stress may develop as a reaction to racism, including (a) racial discrimination, or avoiding or ostracizing the person because of her or his race or culture; (b) racial harassment, or hostile race-based physical or verbal assaults; and (c) discriminatory harassment, or aversive hostility characterized by "White flight" (p. 89).

When we integrate our knowledge about toxic larger social issues into the ways in which they play out in everyday life and in our own bodies, we can appreciate the pervasiveness and intensity of their impact. Furthermore, Helms, Nicholas, and Green (2010) warned us that reactions to racism, alone or combined with other traumatic events, have the potential to debilitate a person and that failure to recognize the mental health relevance of the sociopolitical, racial, and cultural factors that intersect with trauma experiences for the survivors of trauma, as well as for the service providers, will greatly inhibit one's ability to provide effective treatment programs or to conduct meaningful trauma research (p. 60).

In sum, I argue that the history of colonialism, the coloniality of power, and the colonial difference have shaped the entitlements that people claim; the privileges and lack of privileges that they may have; family composition, life expectations, as well as what kind of potential traumas they may experience; how they make meaning out of these experiences; and how they may respond to adversity. Coloniality continues to operate in our lives through the promotion of cultural belief systems, definitions of trauma and traumatic stress, and treatment approaches that have at their center conceptualizations embracing individualism, medicalization, and the separation of people's experiences of trauma from history and context.

It is time to connect the pieces of these puzzles in ways that restore balance and create equity. This is not an easy task because of the temptation to look the other way, focus on personal/individual suffering, practice denial, and give personal suffering more weight than larger social inequities. Furthermore, the flood of anger, thirst for retaliation, and raw pain make it very challenging for families and communities to deal with the consequences of opening up the gates to develop healing and restoration. However, the time has come for us to develop strategies based on collaboration and equity that will restore healing and balance.

The field of resilience seems to have emerged in a less visible and socially intense immediate environment; however, it turned around the traditional medical and scholarly focus on poverty, risk, psychopathology, diagnosis, and traumatic stress. Garmezy's (1971, 1973, 1974, 1985, 1991) finding that children at risk for psychopathology did not necessarily follow an expected trajectory into illness, and that some disadvantaged children remained competent and failed to display anticipated behavioral problems, began a wave of interest in human positive adaptation.

Initially, resilience was conceptualized as the result of a mixture of risk and protective factors (Ungar, Lee, Callaghan, & Boothroyd, 2005), and those who defied the odds were characterized as resilient. Thus, prevention and intervention strategies were developed to increase protective factors that would potentially generate a better-than-expected outcome. Masten (1994, 2001) referred to resilience as an inference about someone's life based on a past or current adversity and a pattern of positive adaptation to challenges. This is a description of a pattern, not a personality trait, and it stems from usual and normal human adaptive abilities. Luthar and Cicchetti (2000) and Luthar and Zelazo (2003) asserted that personal characteristics are continually shaped by interactions between the person and the environment, and that protective and risk factors at various levels (familial, communal, and social) also interact constantly.

Walsh (2002, 2006) brought a refreshing contribution to the study of resilience by recognizing that context plays a fundamental role in providing opportunities and rewards for adaptive behavior, and by developing a family resilience framework to identify and target key family processes that may foster healing and reduce stress and vulnerability. These processes involve three domains of family functioning: family belief systems, organization patterns, and communication processes.

Resilience has also been approached from a constructivist-interpretivist framework by Liebenberg and Ungar (2009), with a focus on discursive negotiation and culturally specific interpretation. Ungar (2008) affirmed the following:

> In the context of exposure to significant adversity, resilience is both the capacity of individuals to navigate their way to the psychological, social, cultural, and physical resources that sustain their well-being, and their capacity individually and collectively to negotiate for these resources to be provided in culturally meaningful ways. (p. 225)

Wexler, DiFulvio, and Burke (2009) added a community dimension by asserting that resilience "is a process involving personal and collective meaning-making and negotiation" (p. 566) and that there is a need to address different communities' meaning systems that overlap personal and community meaning making. For example, they point at how important it is to acknowledge a group's collective experience of discrimination so that individual members of that group do not blame themselves for their hardship, and to provide individuals with a sense of purpose.

In my work with human rights activists in Colombia, I examined how making meaning out of shared adversity created a sense of coherence and shared purpose, and I called it "community resilience." In the Colombian context, communities and relationships are at the heart of the social fabric, and despite the presence of overlapping forms of violence, what sustains a semblance of social order is a network of social valuing mechanisms by which citizens relate to each other (Hernández, 2002b). A key aspect of community resilience is the construction of collective meaning, coherence, and purpose to create a foundation for collective mobilization, especially in communities where "we" takes precedence over "I."

In fact, Suarez-Ojeda (2001) affirmed that in Latin America the first resilience approaches emerged around 1995 and resulted from the tests that social, political, and natural disasters brought to entire communities, forcing them to rely on their sense of community and solidarity to overcome adversity. Others have addressed the same issues of connectedness, community, and solidarity in working with LGBTQ (lesbian, gay, bisexual, transgendered, and questioning [Doty, Willoughby, Lindahl, & Malik, 2010; Nesmith, Burton, & Cosgrove, 1999; Russell, 2005]) and African American youth (Ferguson, 1994), while Canadian scholars (Kirmayer, Dandeneau, Marshall, Phillips, & Williamson, 2011) proposed a social-ecological view of resilience to address the distinctive cultures, geographical and social settings, and histories of adversity of Indigenous peoples in the Canadian context.

They identified the following processes of resilience: regulating emotion and supporting adaptation through relational, ecocentric, and cosmocentric concepts of self and personhood; revisioning collective history in ways that valorize collective identity; revitalizing language and culture as resources for narrative self-fashioning, social positioning, and healing; and renewing individual and collective agency through political activism, empowerment, and reconciliation. Here, too, there is sharp contrast between Eurocentric individualism, which locates resilience within, or makes the individual the center, and a cosmocentric view, which locates it within communities sustained by coexistence.

Interestingly, in cultural studies, Lugones (2007, 2010), and Mohanty (2003) seemed to be speaking of similar processes in which the sources of connection, support, liberatory meaning making, and change stem from creating, re-creating, and maintaining community. However, they articulated these processes from a completely different stance and explained them as forms of resistance that are not always identifiable through organized movements and that are encoded in practices of remembering, alternative forms of family life, and of writings such as testimonials. For example, Rigoberta Menchú and Maria Teresa Tula's testimonials speak from within a collective voice, with the purpose of raising consciousness and social and political change (Burgos-Debray, 1991; Stephen & Tula, 1994).

There is a large body of Latin American literature within social psychology, social liberation, and community psychology describing ways of coping with trauma in the midst of political persecution and social turmoil that addresses social context and making visible its politics. Most of this literature has not been translated into English and is not used by mainstream colonialist Latin American academia. It is too political. For example, during the 1980s and 1990s, Martín-Baró, with his psychology of liberation (1982, 1984, 1986, 1988, 1990),[1] and scholars within the community psychology field produced a wealth of work addressing issues of trauma and overcoming adversity (López, 1992; Montero, 1980, 1982, 1992, 1999).

At that time, in various parts of Latin America, the local vocabulary used to examine these issues included such terms as *hope, resistance*, and *liberation* (Carranza, 2007; Lira, 2002). While the term *resilience* has become very popular, and the study of resilience a fashionable area of study in Latin America, it is, for the most part, devoid of its political and historical dimensions relative to social inequity and visibility about epistemic privilege. The word is not associated with the leftist movements that confronted dictatorships and aggressive U.S. government interference in the political affairs of Latin America. It seems to me that while the academics in the One-Third World use the politically distilled term *resilience*, social activists and academics in the Two-Thirds World use words like *resistance, hope*, and *solidarity*.

RESISTANCE, SOLIDARITY, HOPE, AND LIBERATION

Since the 1980s, Latin American social community psychology has developed a robust body of knowledge grounded in addressing the specific social problems that Latin American societies face and generating reflective practices for theory building. Although this field continues to define itself within "psychology," it has redefined its boundaries precisely because of its rupture with pretentions of objectivity and universality. At its core, Latin American social community psychology addresses issues of power and equality and is focused on transforming relationships, communities, and societies.

Freire (1973/1988), Fals-Borda (1978, 1985), and Martín-Baró (1995), men whose ideas became the foundation of this branch of psychology, emphasized that academics and professionals must develop a critical commitment to the people with whom they work. Although this short review does not do justice to the vast and diverse knowledge of this subject produced all over Latin America,[2] it is important to note that, through Latin American social community psychology and the psychology of liberation, many authors have addressed issues of trauma and resistance with their own vocabulary and perspective.

Jesuit Spanish priest Ignacio Martín-Baró (1982, 1989, 1990) left an ever-lasting legacy based on his work in El Salvador. His work in social psychology, which addressed both trauma and hope for the dynamics of liberation, used Paolo Freire's (1971) concept of concientización (raising critical consciousness) to shift the focus of therapy from individual alienation to group dealienation through a critical understanding of the reality of war, which shapes people's lives. Through dialogical teaching, reflection, and action, people can understand and articulate their experiences and then undertake a personal remodeling of their lives and their communities.

The locus of hope is twofold. First, by framing individual suffering in context, stories are opened up and understood as forming part of the social ways in which suffering is maintained. Therefore, hope is reconstructed as oppressive societal ideologies are deconstructed. Second, by emphasizing the community aspects of healing, webs of relationships are reconstructed through affiliation and trust, and, therefore, hope becomes an avenue for change involving groups of people and not solely individuals.

In other words, two concepts are at the center of Martín-Baró's approach: the dialectical nature of the sociopolitical realm, and the process of developing critical consciousness that integrates the personal and the sociopolitical in practice. For him, individuals and societies are mutually dependent realities that define each other and the place of individuals in history. Thus, individual dynamics have to be understood within the frame of macrosociological and structural aspects.

The process of raising critical consciousness involves a kind of learning in which people transform themselves by changing their reality, that is, one learns as one gains awareness in the doing and in the reflecting on the doing with others. In this process, people decode current dynamics of their world and understand how oppression operates. This process brings changes in personal and social identities. Therefore, through an epistemology constructed from below with the popular majority, the task is to engage in practices to transform injustice alongside the people who are dominated.

Hollander's (1997) account of South American psychologists and human rights leaders illustrates one way in which her protagonists lead their paths, "actively engaged in human rights' struggles, whose aim would be to address the psychological legacy of the culture of fear and posit a politics aimed at individual and societal reparation" (p. 180). Martín-Baró's work has been criticized as limiting due to the simplistic and rigid analysis that the dualistic and oppositional categories of oppressor and oppressed brings in working with people at an interpersonal level, and the expert position implied in those who attempt to raise critical consciousness in others (Afuape, 2011).

However, Maritza Montero (2004) reminded us that this field, like any other, cannot escape the influences of the context it attempts to impact. She indicated that authoritarianism and domination may hide behind discourses of liberation and critique, but the field itself has produced tools to maintain an open and reflective stance through methodical doubt and a position of certainty as a transitional form of truth. She cited Ibañez (1989) to explain that a stance of methodical doubt uses grounded knowledge to support hypotheses and interpretations, and these should always remain tentative explanations. A stance of certainty as a transitional form of truth (Montero, 1999) shall last until it is no longer sustainable. She added that the larger goal of transforming inequity shall remain grounded in opening access and opportunity for communities.

From a perspective of decoloniality, it is necessary to examine the extent to which the diverse contributions from Latin American social community psychology and liberation psychology use European-centered thinking as points of departure. Some contributions may do so more than others and some may not do so at all. I invite the readers and the scholarly community to grapple with this question using Mignolo's (2009b) assertion as a reference. The problem is not science at the service of capitalism and capitalism alone; it also includes Marxism. The issue here is the pervasiveness of Occidentalism.

> De-coloniality is akin to de-Westernisation. . . . De-Westernisation is neither left nor right: it questions Occidentalism, racism, a totalitarian and unilateral globality and an imperialist epistemology. The difference is that de-coloniality frontally questions the capitalist economy, whereas de-Westernisation only questions who controls capitalism—the West or "emerging" economies. (November 30, *Turbulence* online magazine).

In sum, in the United States the field of trauma emerged within a political and social environment that sought social justice for those whose pain was not recognized (the Two-Thirds). In Latin America, trauma was addressed in social contexts involving repressive regimes and civil war (the Two-Thirds). These contextual differences and the aggressive intrusion on the part of the U.S. government against the peoples of Abya Yala constituted the setting for a critique of the PTSD diagnosis and the overcoming of adversity using a language that reflected the meaning-making processes of those involved in the work of researching, theorizing, and creating interventions for healing.

The field of resilience in the United States challenged a medical framework of psychopathology and emphasis on risk, and opened another way of thinking about children's developmental trajectories of success in spite of risk. This was in itself an important turn for the mental health fields. In Latin America the field of resilience has developed within a Eurocentric framework following U.S. or European traditions of thought, and little has been done to take ownership of the local production of knowledge that addresses how people overcome adversity.

NEPANTLA: A STANDPOINT FROM WHICH TO ADDRESS
TRAUMA, RESISTANCE, AND SOLIDARITY

Afro-Colombian Francisca Castro told a story about how her community dealt, in a preventive manner, with rising sexual violence against girls and young women. She told this story in the form of stanzas and with an intonation that I can only describe as something in between poetry and song. This is the oral tradition that she inherited from her African ancestors and that was likely transformed over centuries of life in what today is the Colombian pacific.

Without going into the origin of the problem, Francisca began talking about how women united to discuss how male sexual violence was affecting adolescent young women. They decided to create stronger links among girls and boys and young women and men in the community by developing a ritual for all young girls and newborn girls. In this ritual, akin to baptism, selected boys and young men became family to girls by virtue of becoming their godparents. In addition, girls were given dolls that became a symbol of their own daughters, and boys were made their godparents. In this manner, a network of kinship was developed within the community to prevent that, in the future, a boy or a young man would take advantage or assault his own relative. Furthermore, boys and young men were given the responsibility to respect and take care of their goddaughters. Francisca finished her talk by stating that creating these bonds of connection, love, and responsibility helped her community to face at least a part of this problem.

Francisca Castro and her community help us understand solidarity as mutuality, accountability, and the recognition of common interests. While her community is embedded in a social context that most would describe as oppressive, if we "retain the idea of multiple, fluid structures of domination that intersect to locate women differently at particular historical conjunctures, while insisting on the dynamic oppositional agency of individuals and collectives and their engagement in 'daily life'" (Mohanty, 2003, p. 55), we can explore questions of consciousness and agency without naturalizing individuals or structures.

Nepantla, the spaces where there are overlaps and the spaces in between, is where we appreciate, are curious about, and attend to multiple perspectives on a community, and where we revisit epistemic privilege to value and support that community's creativity and healing. Nepantla is where neurobiology, psychology, social discourse, and social practices connect all at once, where the sum is more than the total of the parts, and where something new and different is created. Can you imagine how, as the above-mentioned ritual became embedded in this community's way of life, it impacted the community members' own bodily responses, their attributions about each other, and their own social order?

In *Translated Woman: Crossing the Border with Esperanza's Story*, Ruth Behar (2003) helped us understand the life of Esperanza through dialogues that evolved as the friendship of Ruth and Esperanza deepened. Their dialogues provided us with an illustration of how these two women created community, positioned within fluid structures of domination and intersections of social location in which agency and solidarity resulted in a book that carried their voices even beyond the physical and social borders that they imagined. Let's use this powerful narrative to examine how neurobiology, culture, discourse, and narrative must always be integrated to help us develop a synchronistic, holistic, and grounded view of trauma, resistance, resilience, and solidarity.

Esperanza is a Mestiza Mexican street peddler who, as a child, suffered years of physical and emotional abuse from her father. She married while in her teens only to endure additional abuse from her husband and mother-in-law. Within a context of extreme poverty and lack of social and emotional support, Esperanza was unable to nurture several of her children, who died in infancy. She eventually left her husband and raised her surviving children on her own by becoming a street peddler.

Behar wrote the story in a way in which Esperanza's voice speaks to the reader through the dialogues that make up each chapter. Behar is a heterosexual female immigrant in the United States, born in Cuba and of European Jewish descent. In the book, she discussed class and ethnicity vis-à-vis Esperanza's, and pointed out that although Esperanza's story can cross the border with her, Esperanza cannot. Esperanza asked Ruth to write her book; furthermore, she asked her to write it in English because that way she would not be forgotten and because she feared being ridiculed if her story were published in Spanish.

When Ruth asked Esperanza about her political views, she and her son Mario discussed their opinions based on their own experiences with the market of hand-me-down clothes from the United States and what they heard about their government's debt. Esperanza thought that México will never end up paying its debt because it has been negotiated in such a way that México will always owe to the United States and, consequently, people will always be paying higher taxes to pay a never-ending debt; she described how food from the United States is distributed in México and how decisions are made about oil; and she talked about how those in power in her own country exploit the majority, and she identified this practice as a form of slavery. She knew that she and her children were sacrificed to the needs of capital. Her understanding of oppression and capitalism reflected an articulate point of view that inductively connected observation, experience, and abstract concepts to arrive at an explanation of one's situation in one's society.

How do these views relate to her experiences of trauma and resistance? Imagine her as a child in the 1950s, growing up in a society, a community, and a family where patriarchy supports violence against women and children, and where violence against the First Nations of those lands has been rampant, though changing throughout the centuries. Esperanza, like most Mestizos in Abya Yala, is part of the population that emerged out of violence against women through rape and slavery. Esperanza's mother, like most women of her class, ethnicity, and age, endured physical, sexual, economic, and emotional violence from her partner and husband. The beatings were a weekly ritual, and the children witnessed them directly or heard them from the locked room in which the father left them to prevent them from seeking help.

Let's imagine how little Esperanza's brain grows, exposed to constant fear and physical and emotional pain. Her child's brain is very malleable and its plasticity may be negatively impacted by such experiences, but it can rebound (Siegel & Hartzell, 2003). According to Siegel (1999) and Siegel and Hartzell (2003), genetic inheritance directs the overall organization of the brain, and experience influences how, when, and which genes will become expressed. Esperanza's genes and experiences contribute to the formation of her brain and mind; as with any other human, her genetic make-up influences specific connections in the brain, and her experience, which activates her neurons, shapes connections in her brain through the formation of synapses and new neuronal growth. In addition, mental processes shape neural connections, which in turn shape mental processes.

Imagine this little girl inhabiting a world where sometimes there are opportunities to play, be creative, feel cared for, and enjoy a meal, and sometimes there aren't many of these. Instead, there is fear and actual threat due to the violence she witnesses from her father to her mother and from both of the parents to all the children. During these times, her little brain tries to adapt by appraising the threat; for example, when her father arrives home drunk, she feels anxious, and her body prepares for defensive actions through a cascade of sympathetic nervous system firings and the release of epinephrine and adrenaline, stress hormones. Her little pupils dilate and her skin hair rises as blood flows to her legs and arms; she runs to hide under a table in the room where the father locks the children. She sits under the table, frozen, and hears her mother cry and beg for her life while he continues to call her names. As she tightens her body and covers her ears, she tries to think about something else, and, with practice, manages to decrease her awareness of her feelings. It then feels like it is happening at a distance and she cannot be touched.

As she grows up, she learns to fear her father and be cautious with her mother and siblings. Experience has taught her that he is dangerous and that her mother and siblings are not fully reliable. Sometimes she cannot sleep and has nightmares about a monster that wants to hurt her, and when she wakes up, there is no one to cuddle her and tell her that she is protected. Imagine that her siblings are similarly cautious, except for one of the boys;

he is physically aggressive with everyone and, in turn, is severely punished more than any other sibling.

Maté (2010) explained that the body's trauma center is the locus coeruleus. This is a structure in the brainstem that has abundant connections throughout the brain and that becomes traumatized after repeated exposed to extreme threat. By the time young Esperanza, still a minor, is forced to get married to a man who will be as abusive as her father, her brain and body have adapted to living in the midst of violence. This does not make it easier or less painful; it simply means that her locus coeruleus first became hyperresponsive to stress and then her body just learned to freeze because neither fight nor flight were possible or promising options to escape violence. Esperanza could not have predicted how violent this man would become because she did not know that his jealousy, possessiveness, and verbal and emotional attacks were actually abuse.

Esperanza's limbic system is also involved in a major way with her responses to extreme threat. Two brain structures account for her psychological reactions: the amygdala, which assigns emotional significance to incoming signals, and the hippocampus, which evaluates, categorizes, and stores this information. As Weingarten (2003) explained, "Coordination between both structures is necessary for optimal functioning; the one reacts to information and the other makes sense of it" (p. 45). Esperanza's body, like any other human body, responded and adapted to the violence that she experienced at home and later in her marriage. She sometimes felt very sad and functioned as a sort of robot in dealing with her own husband and children. Sometimes, when she had time alone without her husband and mother-in-law, she remembered her childhood nightmares. This made her feel distressed because these memories reminded her of much pain. Sometimes she tried actively to avoid them because remembering made her sweat, feel tense, and even nauseated.

Esperanza got pregnant several times as a result of sexual intimacy that she did not consent to. Some of the babies did not survive due to lack of medical care and other adults besides her to provide support. She felt detached when the children cried and could not connect with them emotionally to cuddle and praise them on a regular basis. She behaved as if part of her heart had been locked and was inaccessible. She became known in the family and community as strong and angry, partly because she had the fire to fight with anyone who tried to take advantage of her outside the home. Her surviving children felt her irritability at home. Esperanza noticed that she had developed fears of insects and certain sounds, but she could not recall what started these fears.

Throughout her life, her inner experiences, as well as her experiences with others in her environment, prompted the formation of synaptic connections, carrying information (mental representations) and energy (electrical firing) throughout her brain. According to Siegel (2007b), the mind directs, emerges from, and rides on these firing patterns. When Esperanza experienced violence against her as a child and as an adult and when she experienced the everyday social violence that comes with being a street peddler, synaptic connections were both made and possibly prevented so that all aspects of an experience gathered together into a neural net that encoded the representation of particular events.

In spite of the adversity and traumatic experiences that Esperanza had in her life, she survived, resisted oppression, and even thrived within the limitations that she faced. After all, her wish that her life story would not be forgotten became a reality, as so many people have heard her story in both Spanish and English (Behar, 2003). In addition, her story also brought a tangible reward in the form of the income that Behar's book produced.

How do resistance and solidarity play out in this story? Esperanza and her siblings survived the abuse of their father by escaping. These children acted not only out of fear, but also out of hope of being reunited with their mother and having a different life. After escaping more than once and overcoming more hardships, mother and children were reunited. Life did not become easier for Esperanza and her siblings, but at least they were not subjected to their father's violence, and this made an important difference in their lives. They had safety.

Years later, Esperanza left her abusive husband and mother-in-law and, at that time, took the remarkable step of going to the authorities to seek safety and a divorce. Although the legal system was not protecting or affirming of women, it had changed enough to allow women in her situation the right to leave the perpetrator and keep her children. She had the courage to speak out about the abuse. Perhaps she had learned how to gauge her chances of success at surviving, in addition to her inner strength and persistence to change her life situation. She raised her children within a community of people in similar circumstances.

Like other women and men in her situation, she worked hard every day of her life, only to earn very little by cleaning houses and selling goods in the street. She also happened to befriend Ruth Behar, a woman she perceived as a "gringa," because in Esperanza's world, White-looking women with White husbands who speak English and cross the border at will are not a part of her world but of the other world. Esperanza's story is an illustration of how well she navigated the resources she had in life to sustain herself and her family and how she negotiated divorcing and keeping her children, and her relationship with Ruth Behar, in ways that allowed her to keep her integrity.

Based on Kirmayer's work in cultural psychiatry (2006) and Siegel's interpersonal neurobiology (2007a, 2007b), it is possible to hypothesize that our neurobiology shapes culture as much as culture shapes our neurobiology. There is a feedback loop that connects all living organisms being impacted by all in chains of events that we are beginning to understand. Kirmayer (2006) explained that "culture is a biological construct in that evolution has resulted in our biological preparedness to acquire culture through various forms of learning and the neural machinery needed to negotiate the complexities of cultural worlds" (p. 130).

Thus, just as what fires together, wires and survives together (Siegel, 1999; Badenoch, 2008), culturally mediated attitudes toward the body shape our attention, interpretation, and response to bodily symptoms (e.g., anxiety) in us and in those around us, and these, in turn, may aggravate or alleviate distress. At the same time, our understanding of neurobiology, health, and illness are conditioned by the culture we produce, reflecting dominant social ideologies. What we call mental health resides both in our neurobiology and in the interpersonal interactions with our families and communities that are embedded in a larger society.

Let's go back to Esperanza's story and hypothesize about how her experiences as a female, sexual, able-bodied, poverty-stricken Mestiza shaped her well-being and that of her family and community. In the following excerpt, Behar (2003) described a family conflict resulting partly because Esperanza's mother gave her a small piece of land on which to build her own home. This caused jealousy among her siblings and half-siblings, and Manolo, the one with the most means, accused Esperanza of moving the property line and taking her mother's lands to build her kitchen and two rooms.

At the time, her sister Hipólita had retired from years of working as a domestic servant and was living with their mother. Hipólita used to criticize Esperanza's ability to raise her children, especially Simeón. As a gesture of love and common practice, Esperanza helped Simeón and Carmela, his wife, and their child by letting them live with her. However, family life was not free of conflicts, and Esperanza's mother, Hipólita, and others had issues with Carmela. In addition, Simeón was sometimes physically and verbally violent with Carmela and verbally abusive with Esperanza and the grandmother. In the end Simeón was asked to leave, but the conflicts were still playing out among the women:

> And, worst of all from Esperanza's perspective, the embers of her mother's anger about Simeón's disrespectful behavior toward her the year before had not yet cooled. Her mother ultimately blamed Esperanza herself; after all, it was she who had brought such a terrible son into this world! (Behar, 2003, p. 195)

Esperanza said, "They tell me that even my mama said I was a bruja" (p. 195). She told Ruth that Hipólita had issues with her daughter Gabriela too and wanted them out of the property. Their dialogue continues as follows:

> "What do you think, comadre?"

"I don't know, but I don't think they can throw you out if you have those papers," I reply, in as reassuring a tone as I can manage.

"But she wants us to leave."

"That's the worst part, that it's your mama."

"Now my mama has gotten turned around. I might have expected it from my brothers and sisters, but now it's even my mama. It's a pity I didn't go to school so I could read better. If I knew a little more, I could get myself out of this." (Behar, 2003, p. 201)

In examining the legacy of patriarchal family functioning, it is clear that, in the end, women are not only responsible for the caretaking of everyone in the family, but also for the abuses of men, and that as both the larger social discourses and the family's belief system coalesce to privilege them and free them from accountability, the women disempower themselves further by ferociously fighting with each other. In addition, Esperanza's illiteracy and lack of social capital leave her in a position where she is ill-prepared to fight for her rights to own the property. Let's imagine now how this intergenerational legacy is neurobiological, interpersonal, and social.

An individual's physiological responses to stressors typically serve in an adaptive capacity; however, if the stressor is severe or persists over extended periods, these biological systems may become overly taxed, generating increased vulnerability to health issues such as heart disease, high blood pressure, immunologically related illnesses, depression, and substance abuse disorders (Anisman & Merali, 1999; Anisman, Merali, & Hayley, 2008; Carter, 2007; Maté, 2003, 2010; McEwen, 2000). Yehuda and her colleagues have been studying the role of cortisol in the intergenerational transmission of risk of post-traumatic stress (Yehuda & Flory, 2007; Yehuda et al., 2007; Yehuda & LeDoux, 2007; Yehuda & Bierer, 2008) and have provided data supporting the hypothesis that "the development of PTSD is facilitated by a failure to contain the biologic stress response at the time, resulting in a cascade of alterations that lead to intrusive recollections of the event, avoidance of reminders of the event, and symptoms of hyperarousal" (Yehuda, 2002, pp. 111–112). Apparently, low cortisol levels may contribute to subsequent biological abnormalities in responding to traumatic events, which, in tandem with distorted cognitions about the world and the self that are present in the home, predispose children to develop post-traumatic stress if exposed to a traumatic event.

Kirmayer (2006) discussed Meaney et al.'s (2001) research on how natural variations in maternal behavior in rats influenced their pups' later responses to stress. He explained that changes in the hypothalamic-pituitary-adrenocortical stress response system are likely mediated by heritable changes in gene expression that may "persist throughout life and may also influence the animal's subsequent parenting behavior" (Kirmayer, 2006, p. 130). He argued that humans may have a similar response to stress and that parental anxiety sensitivity would influence parenting, which then would influence the next generation's anxiety sensitivity.

Of course, this biological transmission could be moderated or reversed by cultural practices of child rearing and by all the interactions that soothe and foster emotional self-regulation and balance. Esperanza's saga shows us how she made a difference by changing the family's intergeneration legacy of violence against women and children and, at the same time, it shows us that these legacies can continue and that uprooting them takes not only a concerted interpersonal effort, but also larger social responses involving access to education, employment, economic opportunities, recreation, and health.

Now let's look at the relationship between Esperanza and Ruth. As Ruth explained in the last chapter, "Biography in the Shadows," her life changed in many ways as a result of her work with Esperanza, which confronted her with her own issues of identity, privilege, and migration. Regarding her own displacement and the contradictions that emerged both in México and in the United States, she wrote:

> Those whose nationality, racial, ethnic, or class position make them uneasy insiders in the academic world often feel as if they are donning and removing masks in trying to form a bridge between the homes they have left and the new locations of privileged class identity they now occupy. How far can one go in shuttling back and forth across these borders without losing everything in the translation? (Behar, 2003, p. 338–339)

One can only imagine how empathy, personal history, experience, and meaning making intertwined and played out in this relationship. However, Ruth's description of her own trajectory shed light on her ability to resonate with Esperanza and prompted her to articulate her own epistemic position as the scholar writing in English for scholarly and student audiences in the United States (at least initially). At a neurobiological level, we know that empathy involves a blurring of boundaries between self and others, involving establishing a link with the other while remaining connected to our own sensitivity. Through this attunement, mirror neurons forming part of resonance circuits in our brains help us create a representation of the other person's intention and feelings.

Badenoch (2008) explained that empathy involves awareness of our own body state, making sense of what we are feeling, and an awareness that this experience may also be happening in the other person. As all of us involved in doing therapy know—as we attune more accurately with the other in a sort of synchronized dance—a shared construction of intimacy and meaning evolves in relationships. Thus, Ruth, as a student and later as a professional, struggled with the different and preferential treatment that Cubans of her generation had in the United States, and with patriarchal legacies, racism, and discrimination in spite of her White-looking body, White husband, and education. Her story is one of overlaps, as she says, of crossing boundaries, negotiating identities in different contexts, and addressing her own privilege and marginalization, and, as she admits, violence too, but not at the level that Esperanza endured. She concluded the following:

> Having put through a personal crisis of representation, I now claim the right to speak from somewhere else, as another new mestiza who has infiltrated the academy. If I'm going to be counted as a minority, if I'm going to speak from it, but in the interests of a politics that challenges the language of authenticity and racial purity . . . Under these circumstances, you become an ethnographer but refuse to speak from a position of unsituated authority, instead, you try to speak from that very *ajiaco de contradicciones* that makes you a halfie, a mestiza, a Norte Mexicana, almost gringa, but not quite. Yet I realize that I will continue to slip in and out of shadow, as I become a non-Latina for purposes of inclusion and Latina for purposes of inclusion, just the way my comadre is visibly Indian and yet invisibly Indian in Mexican society. (Behar, 2003, p. 339)

This engagement, marked by mutual and long-term influence, is an example of a form of solidarity that is reflective and cognizant of privilege, marginalization, and accountability. From a decolonization perspective, this solidarity resulted from the systemic suppression of subordinated cultures and knowledges by the dominant Eurocentric paradigm of modernity. It emerged as knowledge and practice at the margins, forging new grounds inside and outside "anthropology." It emerged as a practice in that space we call nepantla, linking membership within multiple social locations to social, political, and economic resources that serve as social determinants of individuals' lived experiences and identities.

Nepantla, as a standpoint from which to address trauma, resistance, and solidarity, involves unwrapping systems of domination/subordination across groups and within groups, while paying attention to connectivity, interpersonal attunement and neurobiology, sharing power, and lending privilege. It may be time to begin decentering the one-to-one individual, individual families, individual couples tradition of psychotherapy and begin to seriously consider how to create and re-create neurobiological, interpersonal, and community connectedness to heal the wounds of traumas past and present.

In this chapter I offered a view of trauma, resilience, and resistance from the standpoint of the colonial difference, nepantla. I discussed the contexts in which trauma and resilience emerged in the United States and the vocabulary that has been used in Latin America since the 1980s to address issues related to trauma and overcoming adversity in the context of socioeconomic oppression, civil war, and oppressive regimes. I illustrated the importance of integrating the neurobiology of trauma with social location and larger social contexts through Ruth Behar's anthropological account, *Translated Woman*. If the reader is interested in using this material for further reflection, I provide a set of open-ended questions for dialogue in the Appendix. In the next chapter we will review two family therapy approaches that emerged and have been sustained at the margins of the field, Just Therapy and Transformative Family Therapy, and examine how these approaches are excellent examples of practices born of the space Anzaldúa called nepantla.

NOTES

1. For a comprehensive review of Ignacio Martín-Baró's work, including all his works not translated into English, see the three-volume compilation by Amalio Blanco (1998), *Psicología de la Liberación*, and, by Amalio Blanco and Luis de la Corte (2003), *Poder, Ideología y Violencia*.

2. For a comprehensive review of the history of social community psychology in Latin America, see Montero and Serrano-García (2011), *Historia de la Psicología Comunitaria en América Latina*.

Chapter Five

Just and Loving Relationships Heal [1]

When we open ourselves to the web of life, we connect not only with the sufferings of others, but to the same measure, with their gifts and powers. We experience synergy.

—Joana Macy, 1983, p. 32

What does therapy look like when equity is at the center of healing? What vocabulary is used to describe healing? What values underlie a therapeutic endeavor addressing the outside and the interior of a family?

The purpose of this chapter is to review two family therapy approaches: Just Therapy (Waldegrave, Tamasese, Tuhaka, & Campbell, 2003) and Transformative Family Therapy (Almeida, Dolan-Del Vecchio & Parker, 2007). These approaches emerged at the margins of what became dominant models in the family therapy field, and in my view, they reflect well the emergence of alternative knowledges about healing resulting from the oppressive experience of coloniality. However, I am not proposing their blind application; I am not presenting them as *the* ultimate social justice-based therapy approaches, and I am not implying that they are a good fit for everyone. They are not. Furthermore, similar to almost all, if not all, the work developed in mainstream and less mainstream therapy approaches and interventions, we know little about their failures.

These two approaches began to be developed in the late 1980s, and publications in journals and other venues began to appear in the early 1990s. These approaches have been tested by people, time, and space, though there are no large quantitative data studies to prove their effectiveness or compare them with other models. They are rarely included in what we would identify as standard textbooks in family and other therapy training, in spite of their having being practiced, written about, and qualitatively researched for more than 20 years. Even North American critical psychologists have overlooked these valuable contributions.

This is not a coincidence. All therapy is political, whether it maintains the status quo or seeks to change it; these approaches are explicitly political, and they intentionally integrate social justice into the core of the therapeutic endeavor. I will examine these models and explain why they are good, though not exhaustive, examples of healing practices emerging from nepant-la. I will begin situating these therapeutic practices by providing some information about their creators' backgrounds to illustrate their social locations.

In the preface to *Transformative Family Therapy: Just Families in a Just Society* (Almeida, Dolan-Del Vecchio, & Parker, 2007), we learn about inter-sectionalities, geographical location, values, socioeconomic context, and migration:

> [Rhea Almeida] was born in Uganda to Asian Indian parents from the West Coast of India, the firstborn child and grandchild to both of her parents' families. Her 13 aunts and uncles gathered around the hospital bed to welcome her, and the family celebrated her birth for months thereafter. Although they decided that Rhea's skin could have been lighter, they agreed that it was light enough, and her remarkable eyes more than make up for her darker skin color. When she was 3, her brother arrived. Her parents felt blessed to have two beautiful, able-bodied children. Six months later, Rhea contracted polio. For years thereafter, Rhea and her parents traveled from country to country seeking a cure. Finally, they accepted that there were would be no cure, only rehabilitation.
>
> Instead of relegating their daughter to an adoptive institution or maltreating her for being female and disabled, Rhea's parents viewed her as a *Harijan*—one of god's children who brought added value. Her parents' childrearing challenged community norms. When she turned 5 years old, Rhea's father decided that, since she would never marry and receive the buffering experiences that marriage might bring, he would be her teacher. Instead of taking his son to the men's activities, he took his daughter. The men in the family and community criticized him harshly. They believed that Rhea's father, by bringing a girl child into the world of men, was breaking too many traditions. There were others, however, who celebrated his choices. (p. xv)

Although her father's prediction that she would not have a family of her own did not prove correct, his effort to prepare her for adulthood by transgressing traditional gender norms brought much richness. It was a gift to be able to move within and through overlapping border spaces and cultural representations, and she learned to exercise personal and collective agency through her scholarly and professional work.

In *Just Therapy—A Journey* (2003) and in a recent interview, Wahiri Campbell shared insights about his joining the Family Therapy Centre in New Zealand, or in Maori, Aotearoa (Land of the Long White Cloud):

The Family Centre had been going to the marae (Māori gathering place) for Māori language, when the job came up. I was thinking about applying for it, then the marae approached me—"Come on," they said, "you're the right person for this job." When I joined the Agency, it was a real Pakeha [White New Zealanders] agency. When they first asked me to observe a family in therapy, I thought it was like Star Wars—a game of luck and win. It was so technological—one way screens, video cameras. I laughed, but I was pissed off, angry. They were only coping with their culture and Pakeha academic skills. I said to myself. "Tomorrow I'm going to change this place." One of the things that struck me as so strange was that all the workers used to bring their own individual cut lunches. I decided I'd bring along my big port of kai (food) and put in the middle of the table, and if they did not accept my port of kai, I was going to take myself home. It was one way to test the Agency. I put my lovely pot of kai on the table and told them they could help themselves to it. It was to show my way of working with people—sharing, offering hospitality. After that the lunch habits changed, and we now have an account to pay for food when guests arrive, and we all eat communally. It's an important part of our sharing. It's good to have a nice building, but it's no good without people. After some years, Kiwi and I were getting overloaded. There were issues— rape, violence—that need women's insight and leadership, so I gave them the challenge for a Maori woman to join me. So we found the funding and Flora came. (Campbell & Tuhaka, 2003, p. 172)

Campbell has given us a description of how he generated knowledge about the self in his own community and culture, the dominant culture in New Zealand, and the overlapping border spaces and discontinuities between these two cultures as he experienced them at the Family Therapy Centre. This knowledge was dependent on his social location, which both conditioned and was conditioned by his interpretation of his experience at the Family Therapy Centre. Furthermore, his actions reflected an alignment of social location and epistemic location. As discussed in chapter 3, social and epistemic locations differ depending on the kind of choices we make relative to how we use our own privilege and marginalization and how we position ourselves in our family and in organizational and community systems. As Campbell inhabited overlapping border spaces and cultural representations, he exercised personal and collective agency to negotiate changes that he viewed as relevant for an agency serving large Maori and Samoan populations.

Rhea Almeida and Wahiri Campbell's stories help us make sense of the nepantla spaces they inhabited. Let's examine commonalities between the Transformative Family Therapy and the Just Therapy approaches within the framework of emerging knowledges and practices resulting from the experience of coloniality.

POWER DIFFERENTIAL ANALYSIS

Prilleltensky and Nelson (2002) view a just society as one where the bargaining power, resources, and burdens are allocated in fair, equitable, and accountable ways. Just relationships can also be viewed as ones where fairness, equity, and accountability are upheld. The Transformative Family Therapy and Just Therapy approaches assume that just relationships at the individual and larger social levels are essential to achieving positive therapeutic change. For both models, a core therapeutic task is to analyze power differentials. Power differentials are first framed within the larger social, economic, and historical context and then integrated with the specific relationship issues occurring in the interior of the family.

In the New Zealand Family Therapy Centre, the Just Therapy approach was used explicitly to incorporate issues relevant to that social and economic context, including struggles to acknowledge and address historical and contemporary injustices to the Indigenous Maori of Aotearoa and other Pacific people, marginalization and poverty of low-income families resulting from deregulated economic and labor markets, and inequities between men and women resulting from patriarchal values and practices. Waldegrave and others acknowledged that families looking for help had problems that were not intrinsic to them but imposed by broader social structures and the dominant culture. These problems included unemployment, inadequate housing conditions, childhood and spousal abuse, and cultural marginalization (Tamasese, Peteru, Waldegrave, & Bush, 2005; Waldegrave & Stephens, 2000; Waldegrave, Stephens & King, 2003).

The Transformative Family Therapy approach initially evolved as an innovative response to working with women and men around domestic violence issues across socioeconomic strata and ethnicities in New Jersey (United States). From its inception, there was a need to address issues of privilege and marginalization in working with men, women, and children who might be of Color and well off, White and working class, in same-sex relationships, and from diverse faith backgrounds. Family interactions take place within a societal context that teaches differential valuing of people according to identity characteristics such as race, gender, sexual orientation, immigrant status, and class. These social locations infuse family interactions with patterns of inequality that need to be made visible.

It is equally important to identify and address the relational dynamics of both those who suffer and those who perpetuate the suffering. For example, when those who have been victimized by abuse develop critical consciousness, they begin to understand how the ideology of ethnocentric individualism may prevent them from embracing a collective identity and community ties. Similarly, people in positions of privilege understand how they automatically take for granted rights, opportunities, and access to resources that are denied to others. As people acknowledge their social locations, identity, and history, and develop a critical consciousness about the ways in which their social location has afforded and constrained privileges, they become aware of the way their lives and the lives of those with whom they interact are governed by reciprocity. Therefore, helping family members take responsibility for how they use, abuse, and share power in personal and community relationships is essential in healing (Almeida & Lockard, 2005; Hernandez, Almeida, & Dolan-Del Vecchio, 2005).

Almeida (1993, 1994) introduced the concept of intersectionality, proposed by feminist scholar Kimberlé Crenshaw (1991), to the family therapy field by operationalizing it and applying it to clinical practice. She also integrated the concept and lived experience of allies and sponsors around gender, race, class, and sexual orientation to develop healing processes. As explained later in this chapter, the integration of this component in the therapeutic process sets a foundation for mitigating the multiple norms of dominance that penetrate cultural and institutional structures and keep dominant social locations in place.

SYMPTOMS, SOCIAL LOCATION, AND SOCIAL CONTEXT

Almeida and her colleagues (2007) argued that families, like many other institutions in society, share a history shaped by patriarchy. This ideology has privileged both practices and myths of male dominance that have long permeated the social arrangements of the peoples of this planet. Patriarchy promotes a plethora of attitudes often so ingrained that those acting in sexist, racist, and homophobic ways are often unaware of how they are acting (Leacock, 2008). Thus, mainstream family values prescribe expectations that are skewed toward privilege for White heterosexual men of the middle and upper classes, and inequity for women, people of Color, lesbians, gays, transgender individuals, and those with limited incomes. Like Waldegrave (2009), Almeida and her colleagues argued that mental health policy and service delivery do not reflect the range of families and diversity in society.

Regarding marriage, at the core of that institution is an inequitable division of labor that occurs both within the home (e.g., housework, child care) and outside in the community (Hochschild & Machung, 1989; Parker, 2003). This inequity is present at almost all stages of the life cycle because women are typically responsible for connecting with children's schools, recreation facilities, health services, retirement organizations, and social service agencies. They usually manage and coordinate individual and extended family members' needs. When they make accommodations in their work life to care for others, they perpetuate their economic disadvantage relative to men. In addition, women who do not work in salaried positions are likely to be less well off financially if they divorce and will have trouble supporting their children because they are likely to receive very little financial help from the fathers (Caputo, 2008; Falludi, 2006; Gadalla, 2008). Unfortunately, in the United States, economic vulnerability is correlated with domestic violence rates (Black et al., 2011). In the therapeutic context, when therapists reinforce these inequities in the treatment of a couple, they maintain the status quo and therapy becomes a sort of temporary palliative. Almeida and her colleagues offered the following example:

> If a "depressed" woman's husband engages in treatment at all—and often he does not—it is likely that his therapists will ask very little of him. The therapist is more likely to placate him and even congratulate him for supporting his partner, "support" in this case being defined in purely emotional or physical and not functional terms. Male and female therapists rarely define support in relationships in functional terms such as taking responsibility for chores related to other family members or the home. Therapists often neglect to explore the respective roles partners carry or how couples manage financial arrangements. (p. 78)

Transformative Family Therapy and Just Therapy address symptoms within contexts outside and inside families. Both examine presenting issues in connection to the social context that impacts, shapes, or influences in some way the issues for which a person seeks helps. It is important to clarify that neither approach is against pharmacotherapy and targeting problematic issues as an outcome of therapy. However, as Waldegrave et al. (2003) explained, if presenting issues are addressed in isolation, the fundamental meaning web connected with these issues will not be addressed. Waldegrave et al. illustrated this point by discussing an unemployed male client's request for services. In Waldegrave's view, a deep sense of depression and an accompanying psychosomatic condition can be helped with behavioral interventions for some time. But the meaning that gave rise to the persistent feelings of sadness, hopelessness, and self-blame may remain and, along with the political context of unemployment, will likely provide a fertile environment for new issues, which will then emerge as a new set of symptoms relative to poverty. He concluded that therapies that do not attend to larger-context issues "adjust people to poverty by treating clinical symptoms as though they were simply internal, individual or a family problem" (p. 25).

Both approaches acknowledge that the manner in which therapists assess presenting issues conveys meaning and determines the kind of information they will receive from clients. Each approach outlines specific steps to establish rapport and join with clients, gather initial information, and provide interventions. In the Just Therapy approach, the therapist begins by carefully listening to clients, then, at the end of the first session, interpreting the meaning of the issues in a larger context.

The Transformative Family Therapy approach restructures how therapists and clients address symptoms by establishing a community environment in which individuals and families are not gathered together on the basis of diagnostic category or presenting problem. Segregating clients based on diagnostic categories, although intended to create community through shared experience, actually further compartmentalizes one's sense of identity (Haley, 1963). Groups based on the shared experience of a mental health or behavioral problem may negatively impact the identity of a family/individual around "pathology" and highlight experience around "the problem" rather than around alternative ways of looking at the presenting issues.

A TEAM APPROACH WITH EMBEDDED STRUCTURES FOR EMPOWERMENT AND ACCOUNTABILITY

Both Just Therapy and Transformative Family Therapy favor a team approach. For example, Transformative Family Therapy requires a team of therapists willing to share responsibilities and work collaboratively, share cases and supervise one another, treat a broad range of client problems, learn from each other and from their clients, and work with colleagues, community members, and clients who are similar and different from themselves. Therapists work in teams of two or more at intake and during the therapeutic process, and integrate sponsors and cultural consultants in the process. Like clients, therapists address the dynamic interplay between their families and larger contexts with the same tools that they later use in working with clients through the use of genograms (for analysis of family legacies around race, gender, sexual orientation, and class), socioeducation training, and supervision around empowerment and accountability in their own families.

This approach emphasizes (a) the development of critical consciousness, accountability, and empowerment; (b) valuing historical information; (c) locating therapists' narratives within the crucible of societal power dynamics; and (d) developing collaborative learning processes within communities. Although other family therapy models may focus on each of these areas separately (Gosling & Zangari, 1996; Luepnitz, 1988), Transformative Family Therapy focuses on these areas collectively and systematically (Hernandez, 2004; L. Brown, 2008; Brown & Perry, 2011).

Just Therapy uses a team approach to working with families as well as an organizational structure to develop internal cooperation and accountability. In their paper "Cultural and Gender Accountability: The Just Therapy Approach," Tamasese and Waldegrave (2003) explained that their Family Therapy Centre sought to responsibly address institutional and individual bias relative to gender and culture resulting from people's own histories and socialization. They were concerned with the "liberal therapeutic environment where such claims are often acknowledged, but subtly avoided" (p. 85) and where they identified that common responses on the part of those in privileged social locations included paralyzing guilt and shame, distancing themselves from their social location to avoid identifying privilege taken for granted, and patronizing those in marginalized positions.

The Centre has three cultural sections, or caucuses: Maori, Pacific Island, and Pakeha (White). The latter is part of the dominant culture and is thus accountable to the other two sections. In addition, it has women's and men's caucuses, and a similar general expectation of accountability is laid on the men's caucus. These groups allow collective voices to speak as one and highlight the concerns of marginalized groups so that "their needs are not lost in a compromised partnership" (p. 87); accountability is defined as an act of humility. All groups follow, more or less, the same process. When members of a group or caucus have an issue, institutional space is created for listening to that issue and allowing clarification on all sides. Then the members work toward "converging meaning," a process in which those about whom the issue was raised listen as openly as possible and authenticate with integrity aspects of the issue that they recognize as having taken place. This is often a difficult process—especially for therapists:

> Most White therapists and most male therapists, for example, would avow anti-racist and anti-sexist practices. The difficulty they have in practice is that they seldom experience what discriminated people experience. Furthermore, they are seldom in situations where they are required to respond to the issues raised by a caucus of colleagues with stories that are very different from their own. (p. 87)

In these caucuses the therapists are committed to addressing issues with the same care and sensitivity that they would exhibit in their therapist roles. This creates a framework of care and professionalism to address the issues discussed and the emotional pain that may have emerged. Discussions about the colonizing and patriarchal influences permeating the issues raised are discussed as well as the multiple meanings that people give to the same events. Then they dialogue about new practices that usually go beyond the individual and have a collective dimension. They have found that the use of this process has increased their groups' trust, creativity, and sense of wholeness.

All therapeutic work involving someone from the Maori or Pacific Island communities is accountable directly to that cultural section, and gender work, including what is carried out in men's groups is accountable to the women in the centre. Just Therapy uses respected community members trained in therapy as cultural consultants:

> The expertise of the cultural consultant appropriately deters the clinical consultant from intercultural ascriptions of meanings. The particular meaning sys-

tems of the particular cultural group then becomes increasingly differentiated from the dominant meaning systems. Eventually the cultural consultant becomes clinical and cultural consultant. As is sometimes said in New Zealand: *A Maori can always learn to be a psychologist, but a psychologist cannot learn to be Maori.* And we could add, *but a psychologist can learn to respect and be sensitive to things Maori, or Samoan or Black or Hispanic, or Australian Aboriginal and so on.* (Waldegrave et al., 2003, p. 40)

These approaches redefine the role of therapists, requiring that they expand their focus beyond the individual and beyond household connections and blood relationships. Therapists face the challenge of helping clients to construct couple partnerships and families governed by just values and to help ensure that communities sustain these values.

REDEFINITION OF THE ROLE OF THE THERAPIST

New Zealand/Aotearoa, like many other countries around the world and certainly like many of the nation states of Abya Yala, has suffered its share of economic struggles, resulting in high poverty rates, unemployment, increased violence, and cuts in social services. Its people have also been severely burdened by a legacy of colonization involving racism and violence against women. Tamasese and Waldegrave (2008) recalled 1991 as a particularly trying year because they found themselves having to serve families suffering increased psychosomatic illnesses, violence, depression, delinquency, psychosis, marital and parental stress, and school problems.

These therapists knew that the challenges were connected to a larger social and economic structural adjustment program initiated by the neoliberal government of New Zealand that led to ruthlessly rising levels of poverty, deprivation, and other inequalities. They became involved in examining the housing crisis of the Maori and developed policy recommendations for the Centre for Housing Research, Aotearoa/New Zealand (Waldegrave, King, Walker, & Fizgerlad, 2006).

Waldegrave (2003) called therapists "thermometers of pain" because they are in constant contact with the sadness, challenges, and symptoms that their communities, or the communities in which they work, experience. In this role, therapists have a responsibility to publish and publicize both the challenges and the achievements of communities to impact public policy. In the Just Therapy approach, therapists not only work in teams to address cultural and gender inclusion but also engage in many other activities to impact social policy and the well-being of their communities, which are not considered therapeutic by Western standards.

The Transfromative Family Approach uses a community of therapists committed to personal, familial, and community change in which therapists learn from each other and from their clients, and share space with colleagues and community members. Therapists and therapists in training experience the sharing of power as they create solutions, but this knowledge is launched from a position of knowledge building and knowledge gathering. Furthermore, this therapy approach challenges the dichotomy between clinical and advocacy work because developing critical consciousness is seen as an ongoing task for everyone (therapists, clients, sponsors, and cultural consultants). The ability to critically question "reality" develops through a process of learning with others and through the transformation of one's beliefs and experiences with others.

For example, community members who trained in this model launched a nonprofit organization, the Alliance for Racial and Social Justice (ARSJ), to promote community safety and accountability, with a focus on mental health and gang-involved youth and court-based services. Some of their projects included monitoring court-based domestic violence hearings in New Brunswick, New Jersey, United States, and partnering with disaffected youth on voter registration drives in policed communities (Alliance for Racial and Social Justice, 2010).

Another ongoing effort has involved implementing a borderland knowledge-building space between scholars, clinicians, activists, and students. The Liberation-Based Healing Conference is an initiative that began in 2005 and has been led by a group of therapists, activists, and scholars. They invited a panel of well-known professionals (none of whom were paid to do keynote speeches) to briefly present their therapy models and then talk about how these models address social justice issues, all while highlighting issues of power, identity, empowerment, accountability, and healing. Then the audience was invited to respond to the panel in small groups. An exchange of ideas between the panelists and the audience followed.

The first day included only professionals so as to maintain a boundary regarding the presentation of clinical material; the second day included community members and activists who participated in discussions and offered their own workshops with a platform to raise critical questions about the first day's presentations. In addition, participatory theater activities were integrated to address various learning channels (Almeida, Hernandez-Wolfe, Dressner, & Brown, 2010).

In the Transformative Family Therapy approach, client participation in a therapeutic community is central to the process of change. Experienced clients are invited to sponsor newer clients in specific areas and at various points in time because the approach seeks to facilitate changes not only in individual clients, but also in a community of clients.

These approaches seem to fall within a view of love grounded in mutuality and interdependence. Darder and Mirón (2006) conceived it as a political principle through which we struggle to create mutually life-enhancing opportunities for all people. . . . Such an emancipatory love allows us to realize our nature in a way that allows others to do so as well. Inherent in such a love is the understanding that we are not at liberty to be violent, authoritarian, or self-seeking. (p. 150)

This, of course, is an ideal to strive for, as we all know the actual performance of therapeutic endeavors in everyday life involves human agency and the messiness of real life in ways that are complex and contradictory.

JUST THERAPY

Just Therapy is a reflective approach that aims to integrate the gender, cultural, social, and economic contexts of lived experience. It is just because it seeks to demystify and simplify therapeutic practices and roles and to redefine them in ways that can be practiced by a wider range of people, for example, those with certain skills and community experience or cultural knowledge. In addition to justice and simplicity, spirituality is a key dimension of this approach. Therapy is considered a sacred endeavor and people's pain is worthy of being honored in the therapeutic relationship. Waldegrave (2003) explained:

Since spirituality informs every aspect of life in Maori and Pacific Island cultures, it naturally plays an important role in a great deal of our work. Instead of the traditional European dualistic world view that separates physical and spiritual values, we have learned to respect the sacredness of all life. Spirituality for us is not centered on organized religion, but on the essential quality of relationships, and refers to the relationship between people and their environment, people and other people, people and their heritage, and people and the numinous. (p. 6)

At its core, this approach focuses on the ways in which people give meaning to experience and define "their realities." It seeks to integrate gender and cultural and socioeconomic contexts that are relative to the presenting issues. Therapists "engage authentically with people's woven pattern of meaning, and then in appropriate ways weave new threads of resolution and hope that blend with, but nevertheless change, the problem-centered design" (p. 21). Themes of liberation and self-determination underlie the therapists' meaning web instead of themes associated with internal explanations, dependency, and self-blame.

Culture

"Culture" refers to the fluid, yet stable, set of beliefs, practices, and values that a community shares throughout a common history and space. It is contextual, emergent, transformation, political, and performed; that is, we perform our cultural beliefs, practices, and values in our personal lives as we move in time and space. Each of our performances is both unique and embedded in larger social systems of meaning and practice that we nurture and that nurture us. We gather narrative threads, symbols, and possibilities from the larger social context. Therefore, gaining competence in a culture may not really be possible. We learn to be a part of what we call "culture" by lived experience and continued immersion.

The Just Therapy team believes that people who bear a particular culture may best articulate the processes and nuances of that culture. Because their work evolved in the borderlands overlapped by three different cultures, Maori, Polynesian, and Pakeha, the therapists decided to let the people in these communities lead the way in developing therapeutic practices to work with people from these communities. This is a similar idea to Transformative Family Therapy's use of sponsors and allies, since the purpose is to mitigate the domination of European values and social structures in New Zealand and to foster personal and collective agency. The Just Therapy approach is flexible so as to identify and integrate the ancient and contemporary healing practices of the Maori and Polynesian communities. Thus, professional therapists working in communities different from their own must work in collaboration and defer to colleagues who were born and raised in these communities. Community therapists must control the work done with their communities to affirm and preserve their own meaning patterns.

One of the most interesting consequences of this political and therapeutic stance is the metaperspective that emerges out of cultural difference when the impact of oppression is intentionally circumvented by a system of healing like this. Waldegrave (2003) explained:

> The accentuation of cultural meaning and cultural difference also inspires reflection on Western meaning systems and processes. It offers a critical contrast to assess major issues like: cooperation as against individualistic, competitive self-determination; subtle indirect and circular processes of interviewing as opposed to direct and linear ones; traditional spiritual and ecological responses as opposed to a dualistic world view with a separation of physical and spiritual values; and so on. We found that, as a result of this work, we have both identified much more clearly key concepts of Western meaning systems, and received alternative concepts and processes that have informed and improved our therapy with European families. (p. 22)

Socioeconomic Context

Larger social problems such as unemployment, lack of adequate housing, inadequate health services and education, high cost of transportation, and forced displacement impact the wellness of communities, families, and individuals. Waldegrave et al. (2003) insisted that "if these problems are isolated from that context and its related meaning, then the therapist has acted politically to silence the voice and understanding" (p. 27) of those who are directly impacted by these larger social inequities. The Just Therapy approach situates clients' issues in context to develop new threads of meaning that will give clients strength. The idea is for clients to develop an understanding that locates aspects of the problem beyond themselves; their sense of internal defeat and hopelessness is thus transformed into anger, hope, possibility, and strength.

Gender Identity and Sexual Orientation

Attention to gender identity and sexual orientation follows the same logic as that used when considering culture and socioeconomic contexts. This does not mean that the overlapping of culture and economics with gender identity and sexual orientation will not present gaps, ambiguities, and contradictions. The effort to dismantle patriarchy to create equity around gender and sexual orientation requires continual monitoring because everyone grows up in a socially gendered environment and cannot escape the myriad ways in which gender privilege is enacted. At the Family Centre, oversight of work highlighting these issues is in the hands of women because "patriarchy requires continual monitoring" as we all have "grown up socially gendered" (Waldegrave, 2003, p. 36). For example, in their work with men who abuse women and children, they focus primarily on the abuse, its consequences, and on developing safety and liberation for the victims. After change has been accomplished in this regard, they begin to focus on the experiences of victimhood that a perpetrator of violence may have endured throughout his life.

THE JUST THERAPY PROCESS

The following example is taken from a description of the model published in the collection of papers from the Just Therapy team (Waldegrave et al., 2003).[2] Therapy begins with appropriate greetings and introductions, depending on the cultural group. Then the interview begins with an intentional effort from the therapists to create an environment of calmness and safety, respect, and genuine interest. The team invites the clients' stories with direct, open-ended questions such as, "Well, what's brought you along here today?" The therapists try to observe and encourage the development of the story and articulate its meaning. Therapists are not supposed to interpret, congratulate, or interfere with the clients' storytelling at this stage, but to carefully phrase their questions to foster articulation of events and the meaning that clients give to these events. There is an emphasis on *what* and *how* questions, and some of these questions may bring out gender, cultural, and socioeconomic contexts and meanings. For example, exploring how other family members, including extended family, reacted to the problem, whom clients went to for advice, the reasons for events, understandings of what has happened, and significance given to events, reveal the gender, socioeconomic, and cultural ascriptions of meaning conveyed by clients.

After concluding this part of the session, the therapists leave the clients to reflect by themselves, or one of the therapists who has been observing the session joins the clients in their reflection. A team of therapists analyzes each story and discusses the impact of the problem and its weight in all areas of family life. The therapists then weave new threads of meaning to loosen the rigid problem-centered pattern and create alternative meanings to foster resolution and hope. They prepare a message or reflection for the clients. The interview ends with this message, and no attempts are made to discuss it as it is designed to arrest the domination of the problem by the surprising appearance of an alternative creation of reality around the same events. If there have been boundary violations between family members, this is addressed in the session.

Like other family therapy approaches, Just Therapy uses positive connotations and tries to identify exceptions to the problem; therapists point at competence and contradictions in the problem story and use the clients' metaphors to expand meaning related to the problem issues. The sessions that follow pursue the development of meaning among family members. Therapists persistently track events and meaning given to events with *what* and *how* questions; they highlight differences in meaning and behavior between sessions and offer congratulations at the end to increase the impact of therapy. They consider that the real work of therapy takes place in clients' lives between interviews. The following example illustrates a message given to a family during a first interview at the Family Centre.

A Samoan family was referred by the Department of Social Welfare because James, age 14, was assigned to the department's children's home. The parents were charged with not taking proper care of their son, based on his truancy, running away from home, and incidents of breaking and entering local businesses. The father, an ex-boxer, believed strongly in physical punishment as a means of discipline for the children. He also used to drink and scare his wife and children when under the influence. However, this was an immigrant family who had to transition from living within an extended family situation to a nuclear family situation. The parents were struggling with English and the children adapted faster to life in the new environment. Taimalie Kiwi Tamasese led the work with this family, collaborating with two Samoan workers. They delivered the first-session message:

> The team has listened very closely to all the things that you have said. They were very moved by your honesty and your openness, and by your tears of pain. As a family you have had hard times but they know that you have already started to change these and that you want to find love and happiness again together.
>
> Samu (father), the team knows how important it is for you to have a good family name. They also know that some of your children have hurt you. You have thought about this a lot and have tried to make some changes to help all your family. Not only have you tried to get James to be good and to do what you want him to do, but you have also cut down a lot of your own drinking for the sake of your kids and your family. The team was really happy that you have made these changes.
>
> Sieni (mother), the team understood how much you care for all your children and your husband. They thought you were a hard-working good mother who prays for all her children. They know that you have reached the point of nearly giving up with James at times, but you are still here with your family because you wanted to know what to do best for them.
>
> Winnie and Annie (sisters), the team could tell that you cared a lot for your family and want things to come right. Your tears, Winnie, showed us your love.
>
> As a family, you still have some problems. The changes that have taken place will need to go on. And some of you in the family seem to be quite lonely. We think that you have enough alofa [a Samoan word that refers to very deep, committed, and sacrificial love] and strength in your family to make these problems come right and be happy, with some help from all of us working together. (p. 47)

The purpose of this message was to offer an alternative meaning to the events that brought them to therapy and to counteract the humiliation and negative evaluation that the court and the Department of Welfare offered this family. The message given to this family during the second interview acknowledged the parents' place in the family hierarchy, linked trust and responsibility, and addressed gender issues in a culturally appropriate manner:

> The team was very impressed with all the changes that have occurred in your family since they last saw you.
>
> Sieni, the team noted that you have decided to trust your children more. You are letting them take care of themselves more as they grow up. They know that you know that if you and Samu trust them, then they are more likely to be responsible for themselves. They heard you say how very proud about your kids you are. They also wanted you to know that they understood how you have been hurt in the past by Samu and still have to talk about that at times like this. Despite all these things, you still love him and your family very much and that is why you are still with them.

Samu, the team has heard today from you, and all the members of your family, about your changes. They know that you know just how dangerous your drinking has been to the family. Your family can smile again now that you don't come home drunk. Because you have succeeded in this, your children and your wife are not afraid of you like they used to be. They want to talk with you now. The team was very impressed with the way you did not interrupt Sieni to defend yourself when she wanted to talk about those bad times from the past. They think the most important thing you said today was near the end when you said, "Now I do not want to give a hiding, I want to talk." They thought that was wonderful. Winnie and James, we know it's being a long time for you here today, but we think you understand that these times help make things for your family better. The team thinks you must love your parents very much, both mother and father, because you have begun to speak more freely with them very quickly. As they have trusted you and let you go out, you have stopped being afraid and got closer to them. You are beginning to trust each other. And the team knows that all you know that this is the start of a good and happy family life.

The team understands that the court case next Monday is a worry for you. They want to say that they think that you are making the right preparations for a new beginning as a family together. They think you can begin to feel confident and sure about the future. (p. 50)

Tamasese explained that Sieni was addressed first, and her pain resulting from Samu's drinking and violence was identified as legitimate and acknowledged. At the same time, Samu was reminded of the impact of his behavior and his motivation for change was acknowledged.

Situations like that of Samu and Sieni remind me of the painful migrations of displaced populations from rural areas in Colombia; the thousands of Latinos who moved to the United States in search of a new life when their country's economic conditions were abysmal and political repression was everywhere. The Indigenous peoples all over Abya Yala continue to be displaced, discriminated against, and persecuted. Trauma is a series of events involving sociopolitical, neurological, and physiological processes, bodily and emotional experiences, and explanations attempting to make sense of them. Samu, Sieni, and their children needed to address, from their perspective, what was perceived as a threat and how this was interpreted, how they expressed their reactions to traumatic experiences, and how they made meaning out of them. They also needed to find a healthy and balanced path in which the parents were in charge and violence stopped. The social atmosphere in their new society seemed to have hindered instead of helped them cope with stressful life events. The Just Therapy approach counteracted some of the negative effects of the new environment.

The Just Therapy approach was developed as a way of doing, thinking, and performing healing along the edges and the margins of political and economic structures in Aotearoa, and it has shown us that other ways of healing are possible. Just Therapy illustrates the nepantla aspects of struggles against colonialism and neocolonialism, that is, the emergence of alternative systems of knowledge and healing practices resulting from the systemic suppression of local knowledges and oppression in Aotearoa.

Some of the ideas of the Just Therapy approach have been integrated in the training and service projects of Kanankil, an independent higher educational institution located in Mérida, Yucatán, México. Kanankil has developed an integration of Western social constructionist family therapy approaches with the Just Therapy notions of community healing and community and individual reparation, and aspects of the Mayan worldview grounded in the legacies, lives, and practices of Indigenous peoples and Mestizos and other inhabitants of the Yucatán peninsula. Their therapeutic tenets acknowledge their Indigenous ancestry, that language and everyday practices are intertwined with Mayan words and perspectives, and that clients' choices impact all of those whom they recognize as a part of their community. They define the therapeutic endeavor as a process in which both therapists and clients together reconstruct order and balance in the multiple relationships that define them (Chaveste & Molina, 2012).

TRANSFORMATIVE FAMILY THERAPY

Family interactions take place within societal contexts that typically teach and model differential valuing of people according to identity characteristics such as race, gender, sexual orientation, immigrant status, and class. These variables infuse family interactions with patterns of inequality that are too often unacknowledged and unchallenged. Thus, unpacking these patterns and developing equitable relationships is key to healing.

The Transformative Family Therapy approach, formerly called the Cultural Context Model, was developed by Almeida and her colleagues (Almeida, Woods, Mesineo, & Font, 1998; Almeida, 1998a, 1998b, 2003) in the early 1990s. It is a social justice-based family therapy approach that addresses individual, couple, and family issues through the creation of a supportive community and the development of a collective experience that moves systems and individuals within those systems through the development of critical consciousness, empowerment, and accountability.[3] The Centro Integral de la Familia in Quito, Ecuador, incorporated aspects of the Transformative Family Therapy approach in their program Voces de Cambio to address men's violence toward their partners and children.

The therapy process starts with an intake in which each family is introduced to at least two therapists, one of whom will be behind the one-way mirror, while the other will be in the room with the family. Throughout the therapeutic process, there are one or more therapists behind the one-way mirror to observe and dialogue with the therapy team after each session ends. This practice helps to develop collaboration, listening to multiple perspectives, and teamwork. Initial information about the presenting problem is taken while all family members are present. A sponsor is also frequently present at intake. Sponsors are men and women who train to become mentors to current clients. They are citizens interested in doing activist work to stop violence of all types, and they might or might not be former clients who have gone through the program and who want to give back to others or are asked to participate because of their unique perspectives.

After intake, families continue therapy by joining small same-gender-and-age (adults, adolescents, and children) groups made up of members of multiple families for six to eight weeks, meeting once per week. Gender variant and gay, lesbian, bisexual, and questioning clients may alternate groups. During this phase, a team of therapists and sponsors works with each group, presenting didactic materials (e.g., video clips, lyrics, articles) to clients, thus raising their consciousness around issues of gender, race, class, culture, and sexual orientation. In their discussion they use vignettes from such films as *The Joy Luck Club*, *Real Women Have Curves*, *Torch Song Trilogy*, *La Otra Pareja*, and *Maria Llena de Gracia* and films based on fairy tales such as *The Little Mermaid* and *Beauty and the Beast*. There are usually one or two therapists in the room and two or more therapists behind the one-way mirror.

The conversations between the members of the group and the therapists in response to the didactic material create a framework for identifying and dismantling oppressive norms of family life across cultures. It is during this phase that therapists and clients make connections between larger systems and socialization processes, and clients' presenting concerns. They use their own versions of a tool developed in the field of domestic violence, the wheels of power and control,[4] to examine relationship dynamics in the film vignettes and in clients' lives. Through the use of social media, dialogue, inquiry, and reflection, privilege and marginalization are identified at the personal, political, and institutional levels, encouraging an awareness of how personal dynamics unfold within social and political contexts. This process helps develop an understanding that the causes and/or consequences of some clinical problems reflect political, economic, and psychological oppression, and that some of these experiences require public, institutional, and internal family process solutions.

Following the small-group social-educational phase, families are invited to join larger groups (culture circles), alternating between same gender (once per week) and mixed gender (once per week) on a weekly basis. Recently, gender variant groups have been implemented to help move away from a dichotomous view of gender and address the unique and new ways in which gender variance creates and re-creates relationships in couples and families.

Intermittent individual, family, or couple consultations are undertaken to follow up on specific issues.

Culture circles refer to a heterogeneous helping community involving families who come for treatment, a team of therapists, and sponsors from the community. The use of this term denotes a break with traditional therapeutic group work in which clients are organized around presenting problems, with each individual in the group receiving equal time (Almeida, Dolan-Del Vecchio, & Parker, 2007; Freire, 1971). Culture circles are organized along gender lines because women's and men's, and possibly gender variant persons', development of critical consciousness, empowerment, and accountability occurs at different paces and is best enhanced by a same-sex community. This reorganization by gender creates a context for investigating the different ways in which dominant patriarchal discourses affect women and men and allow members to share a common identity, to hold each other accountable, and to empower each other with the support of a community. Family genograms (McGoldrick, Gerson, & Petry, 2008), graphic representations of a family' history, relationship patterns, structure, demographics, and functioning, continue from the initial intake to be constructed within these small same-sex socioeducational groups, as well as the community circles, to explore multigenerational legacies within the families, gendered and racial norms, and immigration patterns.

SPONSORSHIP

Sponsors are men and women invited into culture circles in different capacities who act as mentors to clients in the program. They can be graduates of the program or clients who have achieved significant change in their lives throughout the therapeutic process, graduate-level mental health students who serve as cultural consultants, or church or civic leaders who are citizens in the community interested in doing activist work to support nonviolence in all relationships within the community. Sponsors can also be individuals from within the culture circle who are former clients who have addressed their own issues therapy program and want to give back to others and to continue working on their own issues. Some sponsors are people who have been asked to participate because of their unique perspectives or expertise. Sponsors model respect for people who are different from themselves and commit to holding each other accountable in their work with clients in culture circles as well as in their relationships with each other (Almeida, 2003; Ryu, 2010). In addition, sponsors and other clients are encouraged to participate in civic community advocacy (e.g., voter registration drives, food drives for flood victims, and testimony in legislative settings on behalf of victims' rights).

Transformative Family Therapy is founded on the assumption that three family processes are fundamental for change: critical consciousness, accountability, and empowerment. These family processes are intertwined with particular issues and solutions that families create in the culture circles. For example, in either group, therapists might be working simultaneously with relationship issues in parenting, addiction, domestic violence, and depression, while discussing them in connection to the current societal discourses (e.g., gender, ethnicity, class, migration) in which they are embedded.

CRITICAL CONSCIOUSNESS

The family process of developing critical consciousness leads to awareness of how personal dynamics unfold within social and political contexts. It is based on Freire's (1971; 1973/1988) vision of education for the illiterate, peasant, and low-income workers in Brazil. This vision differentiates between what he described as banking and critical education.[5] The former dichotomizes conceptual learning and practical action; the latter focuses on connecting concepts and lived experience, encouraging learners to think and act within the parameters of their own reality. The former fosters memory, assimilation, and obedience while the latter seeks to question taken-for-granted assumptions and action in communion with other learners.

ACCOUNTABILITY

Accountability is woven into the therapeutic process once a foundation for critical consciousness has been developed. Accountability calls for transforming institutions, creating progressive communities, influencing and changing harmful policies, and shifting power *over* to power *with*. At the personal level, it emphasizes acceptance of responsibility for one's actions and the impact of those actions upon others. It includes reparative action that demonstrates empathic concern for others by making changes that enhance the quality of life for all involved parties (Tamasese & Waldegrave, 2003; Almeida, et al., 2007). Likewise, at the institutional level, action strategies are called for to create equity while publicly accepting responsibility for racist and privileged choices.

EMPOWERMENT

This family process refers to the collaborative creation of meaning and the promotion of "power with" in the clients' lives, restructuring interpersonal relationships in an equitable manner, articulating a new story about oneself in relationship to others, developing a personal vision that embraces relations toward and with others, and taking action (Hernández, Almeida, & Dolan-Del Vecchio, 2005). Although the therapist is key in stimulating the reconstruction of the clients' life stories, the therapist's participation in this process involves an acknowledgement of his/her locations in the social world in terms of gender, race, class, ethnicity, sexual orientation, and the implications of these social locations. It also involves her/his acknowledgement of the contribution of the therapeutic interaction to her/his own life. Thus, this model pays attention to the growth of the therapist and the growth of the client.

MULTISYSTEMIC PROCESSES

Therapeutic work with mothers, fathers, uncles, siblings, partners, children, grandparents, and other extended kin and friends accomplished within a culture-circle format provides both the resources and the accountability necessary for fair change within families. Interventions help draw appropriate boundaries around and between subsystems, supporting the differentiation of family members and the realignment of power relationships (Parker, 2009; Roberto-Forman, 2008). For example, meetings might be held with siblings to strengthen or repair relationships between them. Meeting with subsystems within families can be helpful to explore and enhance alliances between members or to break up harmful coalitions (Minuchin & Fishman, 1981). When therapists meet with smaller groups within the family, other clients or family members serve as witnesses and supportive therapeutic members. This facilitates the handling of sensitive issues, especially when hidden issues of power and domination are being challenged.

Ongoing culture circles provide witnesses who will accompany the clients over an extended period of time in order to maintain a holding environment for empowerment and to keep family members accountable for promises made. The result is a community that can challenge misuses of power and privilege, empowering those with less power and privilege while simultaneously maintaining accountability to those who have silenced them. Even more critical for women and racial and sexual minorities, such a process can hold participants (clients and staff) accountable over time to their new critical consciousness. A group (culture circle) structure and team approach (including sponsors, therapists, and community members) serves to initiate accountability and maintain attitudinal and behavioral changes over time.

CULTURAL EQUITY

Cultural equity in the Transformative Family Therapy approach refers to the "systemic analysis of systems of domination and subordination across and within cultures, by addressing the interplay of power, privilege, and oppression in family and community life" (Almeida, Hernandez-Wolfe, & Tubbs, 2011, p. 49). Instead of using the notion of "culture" as a reified category, this approach focuses on the interplay of power, privilege, and oppression within and across groups to help us understand specific individual identities and family dynamics. It allows therapists to free themselves from the expectation of having to become experts in a culture and focus on fostering equity through liberation-based perspectives stemming from a wide variety of cultures and religions, and an examination of power, privilege, and oppression.

Power, privilege, and oppression are a part of the human fabric and are present in all relationships. Power has both positive and negative aspects and is constantly exercised, intentionally and unintentionally in all relationships and institutional levels. It is easy to intentionally or unintentionally misuse it and therefore harm others without necessarily controlling or having direct access to the institutional agents of power and control. Transformative Family Therapy helps clients examine their experiences of socialization through questioning the debilitating effects of privilege, power, and oppression in their own lives and the lives of others to reshape their power, privilege, and oppression in affirming and transformative ways.

A SYMPTOMATIC CHILD AND AN AFFAIR

Carolina and Juan Manuel had been married twenty-five years; both had higher education and were upper-middle-class, heterosexual, and had no disabilities. They lived in between Panama City, Panama's capital, and the United States. The couple had three grown children, Ana Maria (24), Patricia (22), and Daniel (20). Initially the parents sought therapy for Patricia, who finished her undergraduate studies in the United States and returned to Panama to live with her parents. She had been diagnosed with major depressive disorder at school. When just the parents were discussing the family's history of depression with the therapists, Juan Manuel complained that Carolina had sexually and emotionally left him for many years and that he had felt depressed for a while. Meanwhile, Carolina suspected that Juan Manuel had been having an extramarital relationship with her best friend, who lived a few blocks from her home in Panama. Juan Manuel argued that this was Carolina's fantasy and that his long hours at work were simply about working longer than usual. He also insisted that the recent death of her mother had left her unable to sexually and emotionally respond to him.

The parents and Patricia were invited to join the therapy circles, and this invitation was extended to Ana Maria and Daniel, who, at the time, joined only occasionally because she was living in another city and he was studying in Europe. During the first therapy sessions within gendered circles, the therapy team used short films to address how women and men deal with loss differently because of their gender socialization. As part of this process, they also used film vignettes to address gender themes, especially in relation to how their children were socialized, and to stimulate discussion with the men's circle. One of the exercises they did with other clients involved using the wheels of power and control to analyze uses and misuses of privilege in these film vignettes.

While family members were in these circles, two consultations occurred with Patricia alone and with her parents to address potential risk and invite the family to observe their patterns of engagement and disengagement. Six weeks later, they joined the culture circles with other families, and a more detailed genogram was developed in the mixed circle. This process allowed all members in the circles to visually learn about legacies and patterns, to think relationally, and even to learn how to construct a genogram. After several conversations within the female circle, therapists felt that there was enough evidence to believe that Juan Manuel was having an extramarital affair. Sponsors in the men's circle helped Juan Manuel explore ways in which he, like many other people, favored his own desires over those of his partner and children.

Although this was initially hard for him, sponsors played a key role in keeping these conversations alive and nonjudgmental as they helped him remember that these patterns came more by way of an unquestioned socialization than conscious choice. Therapists helped him consider the ways in which he had ignored Carolina and his children after Daniel left for college. In spite of his great concern for Patricia, his relationship with her was emotionally distant and he did not know how to get closer to her as an adult rather than as a little child. He finally admitted that he had been having an extramarital affair with his wife's friend. He was asked to take responsibility for his actions and to inform his wife and children. After dialogue and encouragement, he agreed.

This process of accountability was encouraged through letter writing to help him remember, articulate his thoughts and feelings, and take responsibility. He constantly received feedback from other men, and once he, the therapists, and the other men felt he was ready, he invited his wife and child to the circle to share. He wrote a separate letter to the woman with whom he ended the extramarital relationship. Though Carolina was upset to know the truth, she was very relieved to know the truth and confirm that she was not crazy. Patricia had known about her father's relationship for years and was relieved to hear that he was willing to take responsibility.

As she witnessed her parents working through their issues, Patricia focused on learning to develop her own personal and professional goals and on discerning how to select men who were not abusive with her. Other women in the circle helped her understand issues of gender, class, and race privilege in her life and with prospective boyfriends. Her depression subsided over time as she took steps to connect with people her own age. She got a job in a marketing company. Carolina and Juan Manuel continued their work in therapy around economic equity, mutual decision making, and changing traditional gender norms in various areas of the relationship. Eventually Carolina and all the children engaged in a reparation process involving dialogue and reparative actions initiated by Juan Manuel.

Carolina and Juan Manuel met in these circles with clients from other social locations. For example, Mariana, an immigrant from Colombia, and Eduardo, from Puerto Rico, were also in therapy. They had been together for ten years, and early on they experienced difficulties and had fights in which they screamed and yelled at each other and were physically abusive. In spite of having had a history of academic achievement, Mariana stopped pursuing further education after she finished her bachelor's degree and worked as a bank teller. Eduardo had a high school-level education and worked on and off in security, cleaning, and clerical positions. They lived mostly on her income and sometimes struggled financially.

Some of the other clients in the circle included Tammy and Debbie, a middle-class couple of European descent, and Terrell, an African American male who had a similar occupational history to that of Eduardo. Women and men, separately and together, learned from and about each other's family legacies and issues. Eduardo and Juan Manuel found out that they both had difficulty asking for help and that their fathers had encouraged them to be "the boss at home," to control finances, and to flirt with other women. During therapy, Juan Manuel, who had thought that his class background made it impossible to have anything in common with Eduardo, was invited to examine his patronizing attitude toward Eduardo and his class and race privilege. Eduardo, being dark, had faced much discrimination in his life, and Juan Manuel was initially reluctant to listen and be a witness to Eduardo's experiences. Likewise, Carolina's prejudice against lesbian relationships emerged in the work with Tammy and Debbie, and this was examined along the continuum of gender identity marginalization.

Even today, the Transformative Therapy approach is seen as an unorthodox practice. It is often difficult for people to imagine how to work within a framework that is neither individual nor group therapy. However, like the Just Therapy approach, it emerged from the intention to address such serious problems as domestic violence. Early on, there was little sophistication to understand why men abuse women. Although the movement against domestic violence understood violence against women as a patriarchal tool of power and control, the focus was mostly on women. Interventions with perpetrators of violence were limited and the family therapy field was late to grapple with the issues of violence in couples (Bograd, 1982, 1984, 1990). Almeida experienced a lack of success in addressing domestic violence using the dominant marital therapy models of the time. She sometimes had concerns about her own safety and recruited two police officers and other men from civic organizations to have a dialogue about their thoughts on men's violence toward their partners. She brought this dialogue into her therapeutic work and created safety and role models for men who were abusive. She discovered that when the private context of a relationship was exposed to witnesses, the abuse stopped.

Some of these practices, which emerged out of a need to address an immediate concern, planted the seeds for developing a way of doing, thinking, and performing healing along the edges and the margins of the dominant models in family therapy and other mental health fields. The Transformative Family Therapy approach illustrates the nepantla aspects of coloniality, that is, the emergence of an alternative system of healing practices resulting from having to navigate the interstices of migration, class, ethnicity, gender, ability, and a professional field that offered limited options to respond to the complexity of working with clients from a diversity of backgrounds.

These therapy approaches reflect ideas and practices that seek to address decolonization by challenging the legacies of colonialism and dismantling them through the affirmation of Indigenous worldviews and practices, by examining power differentials, and by creating another way of healing in the borders. These approaches have grown in the interstices of local social contexts, systemic and social constructionist approaches to family therapy, and the cross-pollination of personal and community experience and knowledge. Although I have highlighted aspects intended to bring forth ways to de-link therapeutic efforts from Eurocentered practices, it is also necessary to keep in mind the need for further articulation about how to understand issues of oppression and privilege in local contexts and how to differentiate these views from views of oppression that assume universal characteristics independent from history, context, and agency.

The Transformative Family Therapy approach's use of Freire's critical pedagogy needs to re-vision and reground his ideas and applications to avoid falling into the trap of universalizing a view of "concientizacíon" deemed as Western from the point of view of, for example, Indigenous peoples. In addition, these approaches must contend with the risk of essentializing categories of race, gender, sexual orientation, and class. Therefore, they must localize and ground their practices in the specific meanings, traditions, customs, and community relations that operate where they work.

NOTES

1. The title of this chapter was inspired by a conversation with colleagues Jean Malpas and Victoria Dickerson at a board meeting of the American Family Therapy Academy.

2. All excepts are from *Just Therapy—A Journey: A Collection of Papers from the Just Therapy Team* (2003) (pp. 81–96), by C. Waldegrave, K. Tamasese, F. Tuhaka, & W. Campbell (Eds.), Adelaide, Australia: Dulwich Centre Publications. Reprinted with permission of Dulwich Centre Publications: www.dulwichcentre.com.au .

3. For a detailed description and analysis of this model, see *Transformative Family Therapy: Just families in a Just Society* (2007) by R. V. Almeida, K. Dolan-Del Vecchio, and L. Parker.

4. The wheels of power and control were originally developed by the Domestic Abuse Prevention program in Duluth, MN, started by Ellen Pence and Melanie Shepherd and described in their *Coordinating Community Response to Domestic Violence: Lessons from Duluth and Beyond* (1999). Almeida and her colleagues created wheels addressing issues of power and control in regard to race, colonization, and sexual orientation. Examples of these wheels are found in Almeida et al.'s book *Transformative Family Therapy*.

5. Freire's (1971) metaphor of "banking education" refers to the idea that students are treated as empty containers in which educators deposit knowledge. This practice reinforces a lack of knowledge ownership and critical thinking in students.

Chapter Six

Thoughts Unfinished

All things share the same breath—the beast, the tree, the human . . . the air shares its spirit with all the life it supports. Humankind has not woven the web of life. We are but one thread within it. Whatever we do to the web, we do to ourselves. All things are bound together. All things connect. Humans do not weave this web of life. They are merely a strand of it. Whatever they do to the web, they do to themselves [1]

—Chief Seattle, chief of the Suquamis

This chapter is not intended to give closure to this book. It remains unfinished, leaving spaces open for imagination, dialogue, and continued journeying. My journey is guided by the following motifs: using the embeddedness of our lives and the lives of all other beings in the planet as a point of departure for therapeutic approaches, integrating cultural equity and cultural humility, and seeking and staying in dialogue with communities and scholars for whom coloniality is a felt experience.

THE WEB OF LIFE

Human survival depends on our effectively relating to everything that surrounds us. By continuing to consider only a human perspective on human relationships, power, history, and community, we fail to see ourselves in relation to all beings on the planet. Psychologists, family therapists, and other mental health professionals (Beck, 2011; Blazina, 2011; Brown, 2011; Chandler, 2005; Dorfman et al., 2012; Freund, Brown, & Buff, 2011; Glasser, 2011; Masson, 2010; McCardle et al., 2011; Sugawara et al., 2012) have made very important contributions to widening the scope of relationships to include the bonds that we and animals develop to care for each other and heal.

Walsh (2009a, 2009b) discussed the importance of addressing the human-animal bond in family therapy and examined its significance across the life course. She contended that while contemporary research documents and supports the complexity of animal life and their ability to feel, connect with others, and communicate, the legacy of Cartesian and early 20th-century behaviorists' views contributed to a longstanding neglect of the importance and value of animals in people's lives as well as inhumane practices toward animals, especially in laboratory settings.

Even today, the ideological legacy of the Cartesian mechanistic view, presuming that humans are the only creatures with souls and that all nonhuman life is soulless, mechanical, and without feeling or agency, persists in the ways that some people of all classes and races treat animals. This anthropocentric view appeals to those who want to dominate and exploit the earth and other humans for profit. Though the impact of the historical legacy of using "war dogs"[2] to persecute and annihilate Indigenous and African peoples during the conquest of Abya Yala is not well known (Brotherston, 1979; Miranda, 2010; Derr, 2004; Varner & Johnson, 1983; Todorov, 1987), I suspect that such practices harmed both perpetrators and victims' connection with other beings, generating a legacy of distancing from and objectification of animals.

Walsh (2009a) cited Melson and Fine (2006) as advocates for a paradigm shift to a "biocentric" orientation that includes our connections with other species and the natural world, and argued that this perspective "is resonant with the systemic orientation espoused by Gregory Bateson (1979) and at the very foundation of family therapy theory and practice" (p. 497). Within this framework, she discussed the significance of pets in family functioning and their importance in assessment and treatment relative to domestic violence, loss, and bereavement, and animal-assisted therapies.

Others have documented the varied benefits and multiple interventions now used in counseling. For example, in *Animals in Our Lives: Human-Animal Interaction in Family, Community, and Therapeutic Settings*, McCardle et al. (2011) offered a review of the benefits of human-animal interaction and the positive effects of animal therapies and interactions on child health and development. The authors of this edited book offered insights into how children with disabilities may benefit from animal therapies and how animals can help humans strengthen social competence. They also discussed animal-related interventions for children with mental health issues as well as physical illnesses and problems with school.

Venezuelan ecologist Stephan Harding (2006) helped us take a view of our existence in the planet a step further. He used scientific discoveries about the earth to help us resituate ourselves vis-à-vis the planet, shifting from a path of isolation, domination, and destruction to one of reverence and coexistence. He argued that "science is a dangerous gift unless it can be brought into contact with the wisdom that resides in the sensual, intuitive, and ethical aspects of our natures. . . . It is only when these other ways of knowing complement our rational approach to the world that we can truly experience the living intelligence of nature" (p. 26). In his opinion, a new worldview within science and within our culture that integrates conventional scientific reasoning with intuitive knowledge helps us once again experience our planet as animate and filled with wisdom. This view of life and ourselves on the planet makes us fully aware of our embodied mindfulness, discriminating awareness, and compassion.

In the mental health field, the ecopsychology movement suggests that there is a "synergistic relation between planetary and personal well-being and that the needs of the one are relevant to the other" (International Community for Ecopsychology, 2012; Roszak, 1995). Fisher (2002) proposed ecopsychology as a project for social change that seeks to transcend the pervasiveness of dualism and to critique economic and technocratic discourses in psychology. He outlined four interrelated tasks for this project: to acknowledge and better understand the human-nature relationship as a relationship, to place the psyche back into the natural world, to develop therapeutic and recollective practices toward an ecological society, and to engage in ecospychologically-based criticism.

While some view ecopsychology as situated at the intersection of various fields, such as environmental philosophy, psychology, and ecology, and do not limit its disciplinary boundaries, Mack (1995) critiqued the movement's lack of social relevance and its essentialism. It is possible that ecopsychology may provide people, communities, and the environmental movement with awareness of the complexities and interconnections embedded in the human-nature relationship. However, to do so it will need to integrate issues of environmental justice and oppression through racism, poverty, and the relationships between the Global North and the Global South (Bellmont, 2011; Mesa et al., 2011).

A social justice and liberation stance that takes as its departure point the embeddedness of our lives and the lives of all other beings in the planet necessarily implies that these approaches would have to care about the well-being of other beings, incorporate advocacy and activism, and constructively imagine how healing can also occur in relation to other beings. Situating ourselves in concrete geographical spaces as beings who are entangled with the lives of all other beings on the planet would likely help us extend our capacity to relate, ground ourselves in the here-and-now, transform our notions of self, develop humility, and become more responsible for the well-being of all.

From a decolonial perspective, this is not an easy task. For example, in his analysis of Ecuador's new constitution, the first in Latin America to have a biocentric perspective, Gudynas (2011) asserted that the constitutional text offers great possibilities for innovation, but it does not resolve the tensions and contradictions of the ideology of progress that prevails in the rest of the continent. In his view, introducing the concept of nature's rights, together with the right to ecological restoration, brings to the forefront a difference in paradigm and the possibility for alternatives other than modernity. Most importantly, the constitution promotes a new articulation with traditional knowledge by referring to both nature and the sacred; it provides a framework for basing environmental policies and management on an Andean perspective of the "good life" (*sumak kawsay*), and new kinds of development strategies. I would like to underscore that its integration of other worldviews and stocks of knowledge in the construction of environmental policy is an important attempt to move beyond the West's concept of "environment," as it is rooted in modernity.

Cajigas's (2011) analysis of coloniality and nature invites us to extend the ideas I discussed in chapter 2 to contemporary discourses about biodiversity. He explained that coloniality not only produces subjectivities but also a dualistic view of the social and the natural world that underlies the development of capitalism and consumerism. This view is expressed in the language of "progress," "development," and "growth." The pursuit of the centuries-old goal of economic expansion has resulted in the degradation of biophysical systems all over the world—the result of careless overexploitation of lands and oceans, and the lack of justice in the relationships between the One-Third and the Two-Thirds. Pervasive globalization has made visible other ways of being and healing. Ancestral knowledge of the medicinal properties of plants, appropriate use of the land, and healing rituals of the Two-Thirds are now vulnerable to appropriation and exploitation by the One-Third.

For example, consider the changes that have occurred in Guatemala and Colombia as a result of contemporary processes of international integration, human connectivity, and the interchange of worldviews, products, and ideas. Santiago Atitlán is located on Lake Atitlán and is the capital of the Tz'utujil Maya nation in Guatemala. Historically, the region has had special importance due to its agriculturally rich highlands and strategic location. It sits on the way to the tropical regions of the southern Guatemalan coast. Its ancient trade routes have connected this region with other highland and coastal regions.

Today, trade continues among these regions and others in the rest of America, making it possible to buy apples that Mexican and Central American seasonal migrant workers grow in the United States and corporations sell to Guatemala, as well as other fruits grown in farms in Guatemalan tropical areas by Indigenous peoples. The Tz'utujil are now a part of the world market because peasants must cross their lands to grow coffee in the farms of the southern region. Likewise, the Kamentsá and Inga of the Sibundoy Valley in the high Putumayo region of Colombia have a place in the global economy. Their lands are located in a region rich in biodiversity and medicinal plants. Their ancestral healing traditions, knowledge, and use of plants attract people from the Global North, Colombia, and other South American regions who seek indigenous spirituality, healing, or ancestral roots. The taitas (shamans) travel throughout Colombia, the United States, and Europe sharing the knowledge that their ancestors have allowed them to share with the rest of us. Both regions are now the focus of national and international corporate interests and efforts to "modernize" by taking owner-ship of ancestral knowledge, and exploitation of the land keeps threatening to change forever these cultural and natural landscapes.

Social justice tasks and various liberation approaches involve developing ways of thinking, listening, feeling, and doing that reconnect us with nature and all other beings. Analyses of power in these relationships need to encom-pass issues of identity, privilege, lack of privilege, and historical trauma and resilience/resistance throughout the spectrum of life. This task may be like that undertaken by María as she worked out a labyrinth puzzle in the follow-ing story: María Yaku was walking in a labyrinth. In this big and complex labyrinth it seemed that she had free choice of which way to go. In fact, this labyrinth was designed in such a way that there was more than one way to get to the center. She could go anywhere she wanted within its walls and paths. This is what free choice was about. What did not occur to her was that she could remove the labyrinth's matrix or array of circuits. At the time she could not conceive of any more dimensions than there seemed to already be. What would happen if she removed the matrix?

I would like to develop therapeutic approaches centered on the space we happen to inhabit (whatever it may be for a person, a family, or a commu-nity), on reciprocity and responsibility between the known and the knower or knowers, and on collective efforts to connect with others and remember our histories in ways that are meaningful to everyone, even if the process is sometimes painful.

CULTURAL EQUITY AND CULTURAL HUMILITY

Throughout this book, I have taken the stance that cultural differences are not the source of power differentials and that they should not be the framework within which mental health services are designed. Yet differences in power associated with particular cultural meanings and practices generate norms and meaning-making practices that define what is dominant and marginal, accepted or not, in the worlds of everyday social life and mental health training and practice. The stance I propose is more adequate for addressing the task of healing in social context than are static notions about cultures that require us to reify the experiences and worldviews of people from back-grounds and nationalities different than our own.

The intersectionality framework that I discussed in chapter 3 can be used to navigate the borderlands in that it allows one to see how multiple dimensions of privilege and marginalization vary in context and how one has to look at all these dimensions and their impact on the self and others. Almeida, Hernández, and Tubbs (2011) advanced the term *cultural equity* to help mental health professionals think in terms of our own privileges and marginalizations vis-à-vis others and in specific social contexts. Their proposal of this concept was an effort to encourage a way of looking at cultural differences that does not reify communities and individuals and does not expect professionals to become competent in someone else's culture. Cultural equity, a term used first by the folklorist and ethnomusicologist Alan Lomax (1977), was proposed by Almeida (2009) in the family therapy context to look at structural privilege and oppression and to address their impact on interpersonal issues and well-being.

In the field of trauma, L. Brown (2008) posited the need to "understand how a trauma survivor's multiple identities and social contexts lend meaning to the experience of trauma and the process of recovery" (p. 3) and the importance of the therapist's ability to recognize her or his own multiple identities, as well as the interaction of these identities with the client's, in therapy. In my opinion, such a stance helps us develop humility. In their training work with physicians, Tervalon and Murray-Garcia (1998) used the term *cultural humility* to refer to the lifelong learning process and self-reflection that allows people to let go of "the false sense of security that stereotyping brings" and the flexibility and humbleness "to say that they do not know when they truly do not know" (p. 119). While not discounting the importance of knowing as much as possible about our fields and the communities we serve, a stance of humbleness allows us the possibility to navigate the many challenges that we encounter both in the dominant culture and in the border-lands.

Cultural equity is a practical concept that helps mental health professionals address issues of structural privilege and marginalization in the context of a larger framework. Cultural humility is a way of orienting oneself toward those we are in relationship with, to aid us in being honest and humble about what we do not know. "This perspective allows us to more easily accept the challenges of working with others, without feeling shame and guilt for our unearned privileges, and without anger and rage for the unjust suffering we have experienced" (Hernández-Wolfe, 2011, p. 303).

CONNECTION AND DIALOGUE WITH THOSE FOR WHOM COLONIALITY IS A FELT EXPERIENCE

In my qualitative research work on family therapy educators' journeys toward awareness and compassionate action (Hernández-Wolfe & McDowell, 2012), I examined how U.S. family therapists from privileged social locations understood their positions, and the process by which they integrated their personal and professional journeys to create equity in training and professional development. I also conducted a similar set of interviews in Colombia with scholars from various disciplines who were engaged in social justice agendas.

In spite of the differences in context and trajectories in both settings, my fellow researcher and I noted that as the participants in these small samples moved up professionally, their trajectories provided fewer opportunities to develop close relationships with other participants in less privileged social locations, including persons of Color, LGBT persons, and those outside the professional world. Only the privileged ones who made special efforts to connect in meaningful ways with less privileged colleagues spoke of how these relationships kept them close to their felt experience and issues regarding privilege.

We expressed our concern because those who attain positions of power in training programs and professional organizations (and perhaps nongovernmental organizations) will most likely continue to be with people from similarly privileged social locations, thus becoming less able to appreciate the experience of less privileged people. The social location of the people whom we as professionals are in dialogue with has a great bearing on social justice and liberation approaches in mental health. One can discern a great deal about a professional's preferred communities and ideas by noting with whom she/he converses, who serves as her/his reflecting board or audience, and whose audience she/he is a part of. Such information helps us situate these communities in terms of gender, race, time of their writings, and geographical location, which, in turn, makes us realize how much cultural hegemony is present in our fields and even in the critique we make of our fields.[3]

Bakhtin (1984) posited that dialogue is a discourse that allows for, encourages, and recognizes the appropriation and adaptation of other voices and is characterized by a polyphony of voices. In his thinking about the distinctiveness of the other, he states that it is the very "otherness" of the other, the fact that the other speaks from a different horizon, which constitutes the enabling condition for the productivity of dialogue. Thus, rather than conceiving difference as an object of reification, Bakhtin (1990) asked:

> In what way would it enrich the event if I merged with the other, and instead of two there would be now only one? And what would I myself gain by the

other's merging with me? If he did, he would see and know no more than what I see and know myself; he would merely repeat in himself that want of any issue out of itself which characterizes my own life. Let him rather remain outside of me, for in that position he can see and know what I myself do not see and do not know from my own place, and he can essentially enrich the event of my own life. (p. 87)

I believe that we must engage in regular conversation not only with people from social locations different than ours, but also with ways of knowing and being that are outside of our range of comfort and familiarity to creatively challenge cultural hegemony and nurture ourselves. Portuguese sociologist Boaventura de Sousa Santos (2010) spoke of the *epistemologies of the South*. These epistemologies' point of departure is a demand for new processes to produce knowledge, revaluing of knowledge—both scientific and nonscientific—and new relationships between different types of knowledge, from the standpoint of the practices of social classes and groups that have suffered systematic oppression by colonialism, capitalism, and all forms of inequality. The South refers to the Two-Thirds (Esteva & Madhu, 1998), not to a geographical location but to a metaphor for the systematic suffering produced by capitalism, colonialism, and patriarchy.

Standpoint epistemology scholars discussed the importance of valuing and engaging with those who have experienced marginalization in one or more areas (Harding, 2008). They argued that people in such social positions can offer special insights about dominant practices that may help those in both dominant and marginalized positions. Therefore, decolonial thinking and borderland epistemology cannot exclusively be an intellectual endeavor. In the end, possibilities for the emergence of alternative knowledges resulting from the oppressive experience of coloniality, and for "epistemic disobedience" relative to social justice and liberation-based therapeutic approaches, are tied to local and ongoing engagement with the multiple voices and practices that emerge from and coexist in nepantla spaces.

Santos (2010) argued that critical theory proposes alternatives with known historical subjects; however, in his view, those who have produced the most important changes in recent times have been precisely social groups that are typically invisible to eurocentric critical theory, that is, women, Indigenous people, peasants, gays and lesbians, and the unemployed. As in the case of the incorporation of the philosophy of the "good living" (el buen vivir) in the Ecuadoran and Bolivian constitutions, this philosophy cannot be translated into concepts akin to what we know as socialist ideas. Instead, we find that their ideas are akin to terms like *dignity, respect, self-determination*, and *territory*.

Santos (2006) said that "epistemological imagination allows for the recognition of different knowledges, perspectives and scales of identification, analysis and evaluation of practices," and "democratic imagination allows for the recognition of different practices and social agents" (p. 23). This position differs from the assumption that if one critiques modernity and the uses, ideology, actors, sources, and standards of contemporary Western science, one is therefore taking an either/or stance and advocating for any alternative to replace it, regardless of how disparate it may be.

Santos (2004, 2009), Chicana scholars (Lugones, 2010), third-world feminists (Mohanty, 2003), and the modernity/coloniality collective project have shown that the dominance of narrow conceptualizations of rationality and efficiency governing contemporary technical and scientific knowledge do not capture the richness of social experience, and they marginalize practices of resistance. Science and technology can and should be put at the service of alternative practices, and other knowledges must be recognized within their own logic, context, and utility. Santos (2004b) said that "there is no global social justice without global cognitive justice" and that the alternative is not relativism. He suggested the development of shared local criteria to identify the kinds of conceptions and knowledges that are most adequate to promote social justice within specific contexts.

In addition, dialogue and connection with those for whom decoloniality is a felt experience involves not only collaborative and empowerment-based practices but also the intimacy of friendships and interpersonal relationships that connect our hearts and bring us joy and learning in spite of the potential dilemmas, challenges, and disappointments that are sometimes encountered in these relationships. This is not a mere intellectual exercise because

> Our brain's very design makes it sociable, inexorably drawn into an intimate brain-to-brain linkup whenever we engage with another person. That neural bridge lets us affect the brain—and so the body of everyone we interact with, just as they do us. . . . To a surprising extent our relationships mold not just our experience but our biology. (Goleman, 2006, p. 5).

For example, a scholar and social activist colleague of mine, who lived in Europe and various parts of Latin America and worked at a nongovernmental organization advocating for the rights of Afro-Colombians, had close ties with these communities and friendships that survived the passage of time and her moving into academic settings. Her relationship with an Afro-Colombian displaced woman who I will call Irene was challenged when my colleague faced a dilemma about supporting her as a friend, given their social and epistemic locations. Irene supported herself financially, making use of the limited possibilities that the informal economy in Colombia offers. She sold crafts and herbs from her town, distributed pamphlets in the streets to advertise businesses, helped vendors in the marketplace, and did anything else that allowed her to earn a living. At a time when she did not have a job, Irene asked my colleague to help her earn some money by cleaning my colleague's place. Knowing Irene's history and circumstances, my friend felt anguish, pain, and compassion for her situation. However, she could not change the terms of their relationship by agreeing to a contract that would transform their friendship into a relationship of servitude. She had to find other options within the limited possibilities that their current circumstances afforded them.

An interviewee in the previously mentioned study by Hernández-Wolfe and McDowell (2012) offered a powerful example about friendship, intimacy, and social and epistemic location:

> I think at the interpersonal level it's about recognizing the inevitability that my privilege will play out in a way that has a negative impact. A colleague of mine—an African American woman—says it's going to be impossible for me to be in an authentic relationship with her without offending her. Of course that was hard to hear because I still want to be a good person. But, what I realized was that she was providing a way of approaching relationships that . . . made a lot more sense, which was that . . . given my socialization, given where I would be positioned in whatever settings I was a part of, that inevitably I would cause harm because of my privilege. What that did was give me a deep sense of humility, and I really feel like I try and look for opportunities at the interpersonal level. . . . [This helped me] to be clear about openness to getting feedback, that I have the openness to account for the things that I do outside of my awareness and use them as a learning process for myself, and then accountability around seeing myself in a role where, with other people of privilege, I'm modeling those behaviors. (p. 172)

THE BASKET OF KNOWLEDGE AND THE SWEETENING OF THE WORD

I end this nepantla journey with a description of a metaphor and ritual from the Muinai-Huitoto the basket of knowledge and the ritual of the word. Although my description is incomplete in that it does not discuss the Huitoto's cosmogony, I chose to include it here to honor this ancestral gift and the wisdom of a people who have greatly suffered the impact of the conquest and colonization of the Amazon.

According to Becerra (1998), Benavides (2005), and Corredor and Torres (1989), for the Huitoto the basket is a metaphor for the universe and the divine weave. The basket of knowledge, located in an imaginary point in the chest, is the place where the word is held. In contrast with associations that we may make between the brain and language, for the Huitoto, the word lies in the chest; it is held in the heart. For me, locating language metaphorically in the heart opens up a connection between thinking and feeling, how words are felt, and the bodily experience of language.

The ritual of the word involves four moments: thought, heart, word, and deed. It is a process that begins in thought, which then leads to the heart, is expressed in the word, and ends in attitudes, behaviors, or works that benefit the community.

After a process of connection with the elements and the rhythms and sounds of the environment, a moment is taken to bring one's thought into correspondence with the thought of the Creator, the Law of Origin, and the principles of life. This thinking is nurturing and positive. Aligning oneself in this manner makes the mind an altar to receive the revealed thoughts that come from the Spirit. Before thoughts are expressed through words, they must move to the heart to be sweetened. The moment of the heart sweetens our thoughts to bring healing through the expression of the speaker. The Huitoto do not judge in terms of right and wrong; they characterize issues, decisions, situations, and communication as sweet and salty and hot and cold. It is about balance. When thoughts are sweetened in one's heart they are likely to resonate with others people's hearts and are likely to be taken into their lives. The moment of the word involves the expression of loving words that attract, unify, and construct. At this point, the word moves from the personal to the public domain. The moment of deed involves actions that simultaneously satisfy the individual and serve the community.

> *Otro mundo es posible, un mundo donde quepan muchos los mundos.*
> —Subcomandante Marcos and Yvon LeBot, 1997, p. 9

NOTES

1. I took the liberty to change the wording of this quote so that the language used refers to humankind instead of men.

2. It seems that the Spanish royalty's thirst for the blood of animals is unfortunately well and alive today. On July 21, 2012, the *Washington Post*, the *Guardian* (UK), and other newspapers reported that Spain's king engages in hunting in Botswana. Pictures showed him with his "trophies": dead elephants and buffaloes. The Spanish chapter of the World Wildlife Fund ousted him and abolished the seat of "honorary president" he held.

3. Cultural hegemony, a concept advanced by Italian philosopher Antonio Gramsci, refers to the idea that a society that may seem culturally diverse can be dominated by one social group, which manipulates beliefs, explanations, values, and practices, representing them as societal norms. These norms are then perceived by almost everyone as universally valid ideology; they justify the social, political, and economic status quo as natural and beneficial for everyone, rather than as socially constructed beliefs and practices that benefit few.

Appendix

Questions for Reflection and Dialogue With Others

CHAPTER 2

1. A Look at Your Ancestry

- Does the experience of ancestral knowledge have meaning for you?
- Can you trace who your ancestors were four generations back? If you can, what did you learn about the interplay of migration, ethnicity, gender, sexual orientation, class, language, religion, and the economy in their lives?
- If you are unable to trace your ancestors, how does this inability inform your knowledge about the interplay of migration, economy, ethnicity, gender, sexual orientation, class, language, religion, and the economy in their time?
- How did each generation's ethnicities, genders, sexual orientations, class status, languages, religions, and migrations change over time?
- Do you understand how your ancestors' evolving social contexts and shifting geographical locations shape access and opportunity or disadvantage and hardship?
- How have you benefited from the changes and achievements that each generation brought about?
- Did your generation experience multiple losses?

2. What's in a Name?

- Think about your name. Do you define yourself by your first or last name or both? Who gave you this name? What is the cultural legacy behind it? What language is it in? Where does your last name come from? On a personal level, what is your legacy of your last name? Who in your family chose your first name?
- Are there any legacies that are honored or erased by your name?
- What is the name of the city or town in which you were born? What is the name of the state and country?
- Is it a European name? If so, what is the indigenous name of the land in which you were born?
- Name your disciplinary field. What does it mean? What is the social context in which this name began to be used and became legitimized?
- *Language has the power to affix new labels to old practices and potentially wipe out the accumulated historical layers of meaning from memory and identity.*

3. Representation

- Have you ever seen that the indigenous contributions from Abya-Yala are mentioned in mental health textbooks in sections addressing epistemology, foundations of knowledge and the helping professions?
- How does western science discuss and include knowledge and healing practices of Abya Yala's peoples in research and professional literature? What is the point of reference? How this knowledge is evaluated vis-a-vis western models of healing?
- How has western science represented the indigenous people and Mestizos from Abya Yala?
- Do you see a pattern emerging of how the globalization of knowledge and western knowledge and culture reaffirms the west's view of itself as the center of legitimate construction, dissemination, and production of knowledge?

4. Healing

- What notion of healing underlies the therapeutic intervention for Ishmael?
- What notion of resilience underlies this therapeutic intervention?

CHAPTER 3

1. Hybridity and Music

- Investigate what the Argentinian cadombe is and other hybrid musical expressions such as those developed in the Colombian southern Pacific coast (e.g., baile de marimba and currulao). What are other hybrid musical expressions in your country or your parents' country of origin?
- What do these musical traditions say about the social context in which they emerged and how do you think that they shaped and were shaped by the larger society?
- What does music say about peoples' relationship with their own bodies and how they connect to others?
- A number of connections between sound, neurotransmitters, organs, muscles, and concepts about music occur within our bodies. What do ancestral, folk, and contemporary musical practices say to you about this interconnectedness?

2. Journeys of Transformation

- Do you have an example of a journey to critical consciousness?
- What transformations in your relationships with others, the land, and the spiritual did it involve?
- Have you moved beyond making changes in your immediate interpersonal environment to larger social contexts? How? What strategies have and have not worked?

3. Professional Development Map

- Where did you go to school (elementary, secondary, college, postgraduate)?
- Where were the schools you attended located and who had access to them? What was the tuition cost?
- Identify three instructors from high school, college, and graduate school. What do you think was their social class? What do you think were class markers for guessing their class? What were their gender, sexual orientation, and ability?
- Identify the main psychological and mental health theories that you were trained in as an undergrad and as a graduate student?
- Where were the authors from? What was their gender and sexual orientation?

- Where did you do your practica? Whom did you work with? How was their social location similar and different to yours?
- What knowledge and practices do you reproduce in your mental health practice?

CHAPTER 4

- How does studying traumatic stress in social and historical context help us pay attention to the role that unprotective bystanders and perpetrators play in creating and maintaining pain?
- What are some problems that emerge from viewing a part of a picture as if it is whole and universal?
- How does epistemic privilege play out in our thinking and approaching trauma, resilience, and resistance?
- Does language matter? How does the language we use to refer to certain activities and relationships matter in our daily lives and affect the knowledge we produce?
- Whose language prevails? What are the implications for scholars, researchers, and communities?
- ¿Qué pasa cuando no nos podemos expresar en nuestro propio idioma y tenemos que recurrir a las categorías de pensamiento de otras comunidades a través de su idioma?
- How does what we call trauma look from the perspective of those whose voices did not enter into the academic and professional discourses about it?
- How would we talk about our own intergenerational legacies of suffering and resistance if we remembered them?
- How would our work look if we made visible our social locations and epistemic privilege in our work? Would this change how we relate with the communities with whom we work? Would accountability play a role? How?
- What practices constitute survival, resistance, and resilience from the perspective of those who have endured intergenerational trauma in Abya Yala?
- How would you connect the personal and the collective aspects of trauma and healing?
- What are the needs of each of the present generations (children, youth, adults, elders)? What will be the needs of the next generations?

Bibliography

Afuape, T. (2011). *Power, resistance and liberation in therapy with survivors of trauma: To have our hearts broken.* East Sussex, UK: Routledge.

Alarcón, N. (1990). Chicana feminism: In the tracks of "the" native woman. *Cultural Studies, 4*(3), 248–255.

Alegría, C. (2003). *El mundo es ancho y ajeno.* Madrid, Spain: Editorial Alianza.

Alliance for Racial and Social Justice. (2010). Liberated narratives: Being accountable for self, friendship and community. In C. Berman-Cushing, L. Cabbil, M. Freeman, J. Hitchcook, & K. Richards (Eds.), *Accountability and White anti-racist organizing: Stories from our work* (pp. 180–2005). Roselle, NJ: Crandall, Dostie, & Douglas Books.

Almeida, R. V. (1993). Unexamined assumptions and service delivery systems. *Journal of Feminist Family Therapy, 5*(1), 3–23.

Almeida, R. V. (1994). *Expansions of feminist family theory through diversity.* New York, NY: Haworth Press.

Almeida, R. V. (1998). The dislocation of women's experience in family therapy. In R. V. Almeida (Ed.), *Transformations of gender and race: Family and developmental perspectives* (pp. 1–22). New York, NY: Haworth Press.

Almeida, R. V., Woods, R., & Messineo, T. (1998b). Child development: Intersectionality of race, gender, and culture. In R. Almeida (Ed.), *Transformations of gender and race: Family and developmental perspectives* (pp. 23–47). New York, NY: Haworth Press.

Almeida, R. V. (2003). Creating collectives of liberation. In L. B. Silverstein & T. J. Goodrich (Eds.), *Feminist family therapy: Empowerment in social context* (pp. 293–306). Washington, DC: American Psychological Association.

Almeida, R. V. (2009). Cultural equity. Liberation based healing conference, Portland, Oregon.

Almeida, R. V., & Lockard, J. (2005). The cultural context model: A new paradigm for accountability, empowerment, and the development of critical consciousness against domestic violence. In N. J. Sokoloff & C. Pratt (Eds.), *Domestic violence at the margins: Readings on race, class, gender, and culture* (pp. 301–320). New Brunswick, NJ: Rutgers University Press.

Almeida, R. V., Dolan-Del Vecchio, K., & Parker, L. (2007). *Transformative family therapy: Just families in a just society.* Boston, MA: Allyn & Bacon.

Almeida, R., Hernández-Wolfe, P., Dressner, L., & Brown, A. L. (2010). *Liberation-based healing conference. Liberation-based approaches to healing.* Austin, Texas.

Almeida, R. V., Hernández-Wolfe, P., & Tubbs, C. (2011). Cultural equity: Bridging the complexity of social identities with therapeutic practices. *The International Journal of Narrative Therapy and Community Work, 3*, 43–56.

Anisman, H., & Merali, Z. (1999). Understanding stress: Characteristics and caveats. *Alcohol Research & Health: The Journal of the National Institute on Alcohol Abuse and Alcoholoism, 23*, 241–249.

Anisman, H., Merali, Z., & Hayley, S. (2008). Depressive disorders: Contribution of cytokines and other growth factors. In M. Hersen & A. M. Gross (Eds.), *Handbook of clinical psychology* (pp. 779–809). New York, NY: Wiley & Sons.

Anzaldúa, G. (1981). El mundo zurdo: The vision. In C. Moraga and G. Anzaldúa (Eds.), *This bridge called my back: Writings by radical women of color* (pp. 195–196). New York: Persephone.

Anzaldúa, G. (1987). *Borderlands/la frontera: The new Mestiza* (2nd ed.). San Francisco, CA: Aunt Lute Books.

Anzaldúa, G. (1996). *Prietita and the ghost woman/Prietita y La Llorona.* Illustrated by Maya Gonzalez. San Francisco, CA: Children's Book Press.

Anzaldúa, G. (1997). La prieta. In C. Moraga and G. Anzaldúa (Eds.), *This bridge called my back: Writings by radical women of color* (pp. 198–209). New York, NY: Kitchen Table-Women of Color Press.

Anzaldúa, G. (2000). Doing gigs. In A. Keating (Ed.), *Interviews/entrevistas* (pp. 211–234). New York, NY: Routledge.

Anzaldúa, G. (2002). Now let us shift . . . the path of conocimiento . . . inner work, public acts. In A. L. Keating & G. Anzaldúa (Eds.), *This bridge we call home: Radical visions for transformation* (pp. 540–578). New York: Routledge.

Ascani, J., & Smith, M. (2008). The use of psychotropic herbal and natural medicines in Latino/a, Mestizo/a populations. In B. McNeill & J. Cervantes (Eds), *Latina/o healing practices: Mestizo and indigenous perspectives,* (pp. 83–138). New York, NY: Routledge/Taylor & Francis Group.

Asturias, M. A. (2005 [1994]). *Hombres de maíz.* Madrid, Spain: Editorial Alianza.

Avis, J. (1991). Power politics in therapy with women. In T. J. Goodrich (Ed.), *Women and power.* New York, NY: W. W. Norton.

Avis, J. M., & Turner, J. (1996). Feminist lenses in family therapy research: gender politics and science. In D. H. Sprenkle & S. M. Moon (Eds.), *Research methods in family therapy* (pp. 145–169). New York, NY: Guilford Press.

Badenoch, B. (2008). *Being a brain-wise therapist: A practical guide to interpersonal neurobiology.* New York, NY: W. W. Norton & Company.

Bakhtin, M. M. (1984). *Problems of Dostoevsky's poetics,* Minneapolis, MN: University of Minnesota Press.

Bakhtin, M. M. (1990). *Art and answerability.* Austin, TX: University of Texas Press.

Bastos, S. (1998). Los indios, la nación y el nacionalismo, *La construcción de la nación y la representación ciudadana en México, Guatemala, Perú, Ecuador y Bolivia.* Ciudad de Guatemala: Facultad Latinoamericana de Ciencias Sociales (FLACSO).

Beauvoir de, S. (1970). *El segundo sexo.* Buenos Aires, Argentina: Editorial Siglo XX.

Becerra, E. (1998). El poder de la palabra. *Forma y Función, 11,* 15–28.

Beck, A. M. (2011). Animals and child health and development. In P. McCardle, S. McCune, J. A. Griffin, L. Esposito, & L. S. Freund (Eds.), *Animals in our lives: Human-animal interaction in family, community, and therapeutic settings* (pp. 43–52). Baltimore, MD: Paul H. Brooke.

Becker, D. (1995). The deficiency of the concept of post traumatic stress disorder when dealing with victims of human rights violations. In R. J. Kleber, C. R. Figley, & B. P. R. Gersons (Eds.), *Beyond trauma: Cultural and societal dynamics* (pp. 99–131). New York, NY: Plenum Press.

Behar, R. (2003). *Translated woman: Crossing the border with Esperanza's story.* Boston, MA: Beacon Press.

Bellmont, Y. (2011). El concepto de justicia ambiental. In G. Mesa (Ed.), *Elementos para una teoría de la justicia ambiental y el estado ambiental de derecho* (pp. 63–86). Bogotá, Colombia: Universidad Nacional.

Bello, A., & Rangel, M. (2002). La equidad y la exclusión de los pueblos indígenas y afrodescendientes en America Latina y el Caribe. *Revista Cepal, 76,* 39–54.

Benavides, N. J. (2005). Palabra verdadera en los Huitotos para "vivir sabroso." *Revista Habladurías, 2,* 59–73.

Bengoa, José. (2000). *La emergencia indígena en América Latina.* Santiago de Chile: Fondo de Cultura Económica.

Beristain, C. M. (1999). *Reconstruir el tejido social.* País Vasco: Icaria & Antrazyt.

Beristain, C. M., Paez, D., & González, J. (2000). Rituals, social sharing, silence, emotions and collective memory claims in the case of the Guatemalan genocide. *Psicothema, 12,* 117–130.

Bhabha, H. K. (1994a). Between identities. In R. Benmayor & A. Skotnes (Eds.), *International yearbook of oral history and life stories: Volume III: Migration and identity* (pp. 183–199). New York, NY: Oxford University Press.

Bhabha, H. K. (1994). *The Location of culture.* London, UK: Routledge.

Black, M. C., Basile, K. C., Breiding, M. J., Smith, S. G., Walters, M. L., Merrick, M. T., Chen, J., & Stevens, M. R. (2011). *The National Intimate Partner and Sexual Violence Survey (NISVS): 2010 Summary Report.* Atlanta, GA: National Center for Injury Prevention and Control, Centers for Disease Control and Prevention. Retrieved from http://www.cdc.gov/ViolencePrevention/pub/NISVSpubs.html

Blanco, A. (1998). *Psicología de la liberación.* Madrid, Spain: Trotta.

Blanco, A., & de la Corte, L. (2003). *Poder, ideología y violencia.* Madrid, Spain: Trotta.

Blazina, C. (2011). Life after loss: Psychodynamic perspectives on a continuing bonds approach with "pet companion." In C. Blazina, G. Boyraz, & D. S. Shen-Miller (Eds.), *The psychology of the human-animal bond: A resource for clinicians and researchers* (pp. 203–224). New York, NY: Springer.

Bograd, M. (1982). Bettered women, cultural myths, and clinical interventions: A feminist analysis. *Women and Therapy, 1*(3), 69–78.

Bograd, M. (1984). Family systems approaches to wife battering: A feminist critique. *American Journal of Orthopsychiatry, 54*(4), 558–568.

Bograd, M. (1990). Why we need gender to understand human violence. *Journal of Interpersonal Violence, 5*(1), 132–135.

Bonfil Batalla, G., & Dennis, P. A. (1996). *México profundo: Reclaiming a civilization.* Austin, TX: University of Texas Press.

Bourdieu, P. (1986). The forms of capital. In J. G. Richardson (Ed.), *Handbook of theory and research for the sociology of education* (pp. 241–258). New York, NY: Greenwood Press.

Brave Heart, M. Y. H. (1998). The return to the sacred path: Healing the historical trauma and historical unresolved grief response among the Lakota through a psycho-educational group intervention. *Smith College Studies in Social Work, 68*(3), 287–305.

Brave Heart, M. Y. H. (1999a). Oyate Ptayela: Rebuilding the Lakota Nation through addressing historical trauma among Lakota parents. *Journal of Human Behavior and the Social Environment, 2,* 109–126.

Brave Heart, M. Y. H. (1999b). Gender differences in the historical trauma response among the Lakota. *Journal of Health & Social Policy, 10*(4), 1–21 .

Brave Heart, M. Y. H. (2000). Wakiksuyapi: Carrying the historical trauma of the Lakota. *Tulane Studies in Social Welfare, 21–22,* 245–266.

Brave Heart, M. Y. H. (2001). Clinical assessment with American Indians. In R. Fong & S. M. Furuto (Eds.) *Culturally competent practice: Skills, interventions, and evaluations* (pp. 163–177). Reading, MA: Allyn & Bacon.

Brave Heart, M. Y. H. (2003). The historical trauma response among natives and its relationship with substance abuse: A Lakota illustration. *Journal of Psychoactive Drugs, 35*(1), 7–13.

Brave Heart, M. Y. H. (2007). The impact of historical trauma: The example of the native community. In M. C. Bussey & J. B. Wise (Eds.), *Trauma transformed: An empowerment response* (pp. 176–194). New York, NY: Columbia University Press.

Brave Heart, M. Y. H., Chase, J., Elkins, J., & Altschul, D. B. (2011). Historical trauma among indigenous peoples of the Americas: Concepts, research, and clinical considerations. *Journal of Psychoactive Drugs, 43*(4), 282–290.

Brave Heart, M. Y. H., & DeBruyn, L. M. (1998). The American Indian holocaust: Healing historical unresolved grief. *American Indian and Alaska Native Mental Health Research, 8*(2), 60–82.

Brotherston, G. (1979). *Image of the New World: The American continent portrayed in native texts.* London, UK: Thames & Hudson.

Brown, A. L. (2008). I too am feminist: The journey of a Black male transformative feminist family therapist. *Journal of Feminist Family Therapy, 20*(1), 1–20.

Brown, A. L., & Perry, D. (2011). First impressions: Developing critical consciousness in counselor training programs. *Journal of Feminist Family Therapy, 23*(1), 1–18.

Brown, L. (2008). *Cultural competence in trauma therapy: Beyond the flashback.* Washington DC: American Psychological Association.

Brown, L., & American Psychological Association. (2008). *Cultural competence in trauma therapy: Beyond the flashback.* Washington DC: American Psychological Association.

Brown, S. E. (2011). Self psychology and the human-animal bond: An overview. In C. Blazina, G. Boyraz, & D. S. Shen-Miller (Eds.), *The psychology of the human-animal bond: A resource for clinicians and researchers* (pp. 137–149). New York, NY: Springer.

Burgos-Debray, E. (1991). *Me llamo Rigoberta Menchú y así me nació la conciencia.* México: Siglo XXI Editores.

Cajigas, J. C. (2011). La (bio)colonialidad del poder: Cartografías epitemicas en torno a la abundancia y la escacez. *Youkali, 11*, 59–76.

Campbell, A., Christopher, D., & Evans-Campbell, T. (2011). Historical trauma and Native American child development and mental health: An overview. In M. C. Sarche, P. Spicer, P. Farrell, & H. E. Fitzgerald (Eds.), *American Indian and Alaska Native children and mental health: Development, context, prevention, and treatment* (pp. 1–26). Santa Barbara, CA: Praeger/ABC-CLIO.

Campbell, W., & Tuhaka, F. (2003). In the beginning: Cultural and gender accountability in the Just Therapy approach. In C. Waldegrave, K. Tamasese, F. Tuhaka, & W. Campbell (Eds.), *Just Therapy—A journey: A collection of papers from the Just Therapy team* (pp. 171–174). Adelaide, Australia: Dulwich Centre Publications.

Caputo, R. K. (2008). Marital status and other correlates of personal bankruptcy, 1986–2004. *Marriage and Family Review, 44*(1), 5–32.

Carranza, M. (2007). Building resilience and resistance against racism and discrimination among Salvadorian female youth in Canada. *Child & Family Social Work, 12*(4), 390–398.

Carter, R. T. (2007). Racism and psychological and emotional injury. *The Counseling Psychologist, 35*, 13–105. doi: 10.1177/0011000006292033

Castellanos, R. (2003). *Balún-canan.* México: Fondo de Cultural Económica.

Castro-Gómez, S. (2007). Giro decolonial, teoría crítica y pensamiento heterárquico. En S. Castro-Gomez & R. Grosfoguel (Eds.), *El giro decolonial: Reflexiones para una diversidad epistémica más allá del capitalismo global* (pp. 9–24). Bogotá, Colombia: Siglo del Hombre Editores.

Castro-Gómez, S. (2010). *La hybris del punto cero: Ciencia, raza e ilustración en la Nueva Granada, (1750–1816), Segunda Edición.* Bogotá, Colombia: Editorial Pontificia Universidad Javeriana.

Chambers, S. C. (2003). Little middle ground: The instability of a Mestizo identity in the Andes, eighteenth and nineteenth centuries. In N. P. Appelbaum, A. S. Macpherson, & K. A. Rosemblatt (Eds.), *Race and nation in modern Latin America* (pp. 32–55). Chapel Hill, NC: University of North Carolina Press.

Chandler, C. K. (2005). *Animal assisted therapy in counseling.* New York, NY: Routledge.

Chaveste, G. R., & Molina, M. L. (2012). *Conocimientos ancestrales/prácticas dialógicas: Una mirada desde el socioconstruccionismo.* Retrieved from http://www.dialogosproductivos.net/pages/front/biblioteca.php

Cirio, N. P. (2003). La desaparición del cadombe argentino: Los muertos que vos mataís gozan de buena salud. *Comunicação & Política, 24*(3), 130–154.

Clark, R., Anderson, N., Clark, V. R., & Williams, D. R. (1999). Racism as a stressor for African Americans: A biopsychosocial model. *American Psychologist, 54*, 805-816.

Collins, P. H. (1986). Learning from the outsider within: The sociological significance of Black feminist thought. *Social Problems, 33*(6), S14–S32.

Collins, P. H. (1998). *Black feminist thought*. New York, NY: Routledge.

Comaz-Díaz, L. (2007). Ethnopolitical psychology: Healing and transformation. In E. Aldarondo (Ed.), *Advancing social justice through clinical practice* (pp. 91–118). Mahwah, NJ: Lawrence Erlbaum Associates.

Comaz-Díaz, L., Lykes, M. B., & Alarcón, R. D. (1998). Ethnic conflict and the psychology of liberation in Guatemala, Perú, and Puerto Rico. *American Psychologist,* 778–792.

Consejo Mundial de Pueblos Indígenas. (1977). Mensaje aniversario. Retrieved from http://servicioskoinonia.org/agenda/archivo/obra.php?ncodigo=125

Corredor, B., & Torres, W. (1989). *Chamanismo: Un arte del saber.* Bogotá, Colombia: Anaconda Editores.

Crenshaw, K. (1991). Mapping the margins: Intersectionality, identity politics, and violence against women of color. *Stanford Law Review, 43*(6), 1241–1299.

Danieli, Y. (1985). The treatment and prevention of long-term effects and intergenerational transmission of victimization: A lesson from Holocaust survivors and their children. In C. R. Figley (Ed.), *Trauma and its wake* (pp. 295–313). New York, NY: Brunner/Mazel.

Danieli, Y. (2007). Multicultural, multigenerational perspectives in the understanding and assessment of trauma. In J. P. Wilson & C. Tang (Eds.), *The cross-cultural assessment of psychological trauma and PTSD* (pp. 65–89). New York, NY: Springer-Verlag Publishers.

Darder, A., & Mirón, R. D. (2006). Critical pedagogy in a time of uncertainty: A call to action. In N. K. Denzin & M. D. Giardina (Eds.), *Contesting empire/globalizing dissent: Cultural studies after 9/11* (pp. 136–151). Boulder, CO: Paradigm.

De la Torre, M. (2009). *Hispanic American religious cultures.* Santa Barbara, CA: ABC-CLIO.

De Shazer, S. (1985). *Keys to solution in brief therapy.* New York, NY: W. W. Norton.

Deloria, V. (2003). *God is red.* New York, NY: Putnam.

Derr, M. (2004). *A dog's history of America: How our best friend explored, conquered, and settled a continent.* Rushville, IL: North Point.

Dobkin de Rios, M., & Rumrill, R. (2008). *A hallucinogenic tea, laced with controversy: Ayahuasca in the Amazon and the United States.* Westport, CT: Praeger.

Dorfman, J., Denduluri, S., Walseman, K., & Bregman, B. (2012). The role of complementary and alternative medicine in end-of-life care. *Psychiatric Annals, 42*(4), 150–155. doi: 10. 3928/00485713-20120323-09

Doty, N., Willoughby, B. B., Lindahl, K. M., & Malik, N. M. (2010). Sexuality related social support among lesbian, gay, and bisexual youth. *Journal of Youth & Adolescence, 39*(10), 1134–1147. doi: 10.1007/s10964-010-9566-x

Dowling, R. (2008). Geographies of identity: Labouring in the "neoliberal" university. *Progress in Human Geography, 32*(6), 812–820.

Droždek, B., Wilson, J. P., & Turkovic, S. (2012). Assessment of PTSD in non-Western cultures: The need for new contextual and complex perspectives. In J. G. Beck & D. M. Sloan (Eds.) *The Oxford handbook of traumatic stress disorders* (pp. 302–314). New York, NY: Oxford University Press.

Du Bois, W. E. B. (1982). *The souls of Black folk.* New York, NY: Penguin Books.

Duran, E. (2006). *Healing the soul wound: Counseling with American Indians and other Native peoples.* New York, NY: Teachers College Press.

Duran, E., & Duran, B. (1995). *Native American postcolonial psychology.* Albany, NY: State University of New York Press.

Duran, E., Firehammer, J., & Gonzalez, J. (2008). Liberation psychology as the path toward healing cultural soul wounds. *Journal of Counseling and Development, 86*(3), 288–295.

Dusell, E. (1992). *El encubrimiento del Indio: 1492. Hacia el origen del mito de la modernidad.* México, D. F.: Cambio XXI.

Escobar, A. (2001). Culture sits in places: Reflections on globalism and subaltern strategies of localization. *Political Geography, 20,* 139–174.

Escobar, A. (2003). Worlds and knowledges otherwise: The Latin American modernity/coloniality research program. *Cuadernos del CEDLA, 16,* 31–67.

Escobar, A. (2004). Beyond the third world: Imperial globality, global coloniality, and anti-globalisation social movements. *Third World Quarterly, 25*(1), 207–230.

Escobar, A. (2007). Worlds and knowledges otherwise: The Latin American modernity/coloniality research program. *Cultural Studies, 21*(2–3), 179–210.

Escobar, A. (2008). *Territories of difference: Place, movements, life, redes*. Durham, NC: Duke University Press.

Esteva, G., & Madhu, S. P. (1998). *Grassroots postmodernism: Remaking the soil of cultures.* London, UK: Zed.

Falludi, S. (2006). *Backlash: The undeclared war against American women* (15th ed.). New York, NY: Three Rivers Press.

Fals-Borda, O. (1978). Por la praxis. El problema de cómo investigar la realidad para transformarla. En Simposio Mundial de Cartagena, *Crítica y política en ciencias sociales*. El debate Teoría y Práctica, Simposio Mundial en Cartagena. Bogotá, Colombia: Punta de Lanza.

Fals-Borda, O. (1985). *Conocimiento y poder popular*. Bogotá: Siglo XXI.

Fannon, F. (1967). *Black skin, White masks*. New York, NY: Grove Press.

Ferguson, R. F. (1994). How professionals in community-based programs perceive and respond to the needs of black male youth. In R. B. Mincy (Ed.), *Nurturing young Black males* (pp. 59–94) Washington, DC: Urban Institute Press.

Fisher, A. (2002). *Radical ecopsychology: Psychology in the service of life*. New York, NY: State University of New York Press.

Freire, P. (1971). *La pedagogía del oprimido*. Bogotá, Colombia: Tercer Mundo.

Freire, P. (1973). *La educación como práctica de libertad*. México: Siglo XXI.

Freire, P. (1973/1988). *Extensión o comunicación? La concientización en el medio rural.* México, D. F.: Siglo XXI.

Freund, L. S., Brown, O. J., & Buff, P. R. (2011). Equine-assisted activities and therapy for individuals with physical and developmental disabilities: An overview of research findings and the types of research currently being conducted. In P. McCardle, S. McCune, J. A. Griffin, L. Esposito, & L. S. Freund (Eds.), *Animals in our lives: Human–animal interaction in family, community, and therapeutic settings* (pp. 165–182). Baltimore, MD: Paul H. Brooke.

Gadalla, J. (2008). Gender differences in poverty rates after marital dissolution: A longitudinal study. *Journal of Divorce and Remarriage, 49*(3/4), 225–238.

Gagné, M. A. (1998). The role of dependency and colonialism in generating trauma in First Nations citizens: The James Bay Cree. In Y. Danieli (Ed.), *International handbook of multigenerational legacies of trauma. The Plenum series on stress and coping* (pp. 355–372). New York, NY: Plenum Press.

Galeano, E. (1973). *Open veins of Latin America*. New York, NY: Monthly Review Press.

Galeano, E. (2000). *Los nadies: El libro de los abrazos*. Buenos Aires, Argentina: Siglo XX.

Garmezy, N. (1971). Vulnerability research and the issue of primary prevention. *American Journal of Orthopsychiatry, 41*(1), 101–116.

Garmezy, N. (1973). Competence and adaptation in adult schizophrenic patients and children at risk. In S. R. Dean (Ed.), *Schizophrenia: The first ten Dean Award Lectures* (pp. 163–204). New York, NY: MSS Information Corporation.

Garmezy, N. (1974). The study of competence in children at risk for severe psychopathology. In E. J. Anthony and C. Koupernik (Eds.), *The child in his family: Children at psychiatric risk: Vol. 3. The international year book for child psychiatry and allied disciplines* (pp. 77–97). New York, NY: Wiley-Interscience.

Garmezy, N. (1985). Stress-resistant children: The search for protective factors. In J. E. Stevenson (Ed.) *Recent research in developmental psychopathology. Journal of Child Psychology and Psychiatry (Book Supplement, no. 4)*, 213–233. Oxford: Pergamon.

Garmezy, N. (1991). Resilience in children's adaptation to negative life events and stressed environments. *Pediatrics, 20*, 459–466.

Glasser, C. L. (2011). Rational emotions: Animal rights theory, feminist critiques and activist insight. In C. Blazina, G. Boyraz, & D. Shen-Miller (Eds.), *The psychology of the human-animal bond: A resource for clinicians and researchers* (pp. 307–319). New York, NY: Springer.

Goleman, D. (2006). *Social intelligence: The new science of human relationships.* New York, NY: Bantam Books.

Gone, J. P., & Alcántara, C. (2007). Identifying effective mental health interventions for American Indians and Alaska Natives: A review of the literature. *Cultural Diversity & Ethnic Minority Psychology, 13*(4), 356–363.

Gosling, A., & Zangari, M. E. (1996). Feminist family therapy and the narrative approach: Dovetailing two frameworks. *Journal of Feminist Family Therapy, 8*(1), 15–29.

Gow, P. (1994) River people: Shamanism and history in Western Amazonia. In N. Thomas & C. Humphrey (Eds.), *Shamanism, history, and the state* (pp. 90–113). Ann Arbor, MI: University of Michigan Press.

Grosfoguel, R. (2005). Decolonial approach to political economy: Transmodernity, border thinking and global coloniality. *Kult 6.* 10–29.

Grosfoguel, R. (2006). La descolonización de la economia y los estudios postcoloniales: Transmodernidad, pensamiento fronterizo y colonialidad global. *Tabula Rasa, 48,* 17–48.

Grosfoguel, R. (2007). Diálogos descoloniales con Ramón Grosfoguel: Transmodernizar los feminismos. *Tabula Rasa, 7,* 323–340.

Grosfoguel, R. (2008a). Latin@s and decolonization of the U.S. Empire in the 21st century. *Social Science Information, 47*(4), 605–622.

Grosfoguel, R. (2008b). World-system analysis and postcolonial studies: A call for dialogue from the "Coloniality of Power" approach. In R. Krishnaswamy & J. C. Hawley (Eds.), *The Postcolonial and the Global* (pp. 94–104). Minneapolis, MN: University of Minnesota Press.

Grosfoguel, R. (2012). Retos de los estudios étnicos en Estados Unidos en el sistema universitario global occidentalizado/The challenges of ethnic studies in the United States and the Westernized global university system. *Relaciones Internacionales, 19,* 13–26.

Gudynas, E. (2011). Buen vivir: Germinando alternativas al desarrollo. *América Latina en Movimiento,* Febrero, 462.

Guha, R. (1993). Introduction. In R. Guha (Ed.), *A subaltern studies reader, 1986–1995* (pp. ix–xxii). Minneapolis, MN: University of Minnesota Press.

Haley, J. (1963). *Strategies of psychotherapy.* New York, NY: Grune & Stratton.

Halpern, J. H., & Pope, H. G. (2001). Hallucinogens on the Internet: A vast new source of underground drug information. *American Journal of Psychiatry, 158,* 481–83.

Hammes-Garcia, J. (2004). *Fugitive thought: Prison movements, race, and the meaning of justice.* Minneapolis, MN: University of Minnesota Press.

Haraway, D. (1988). Situated knowledges: The science question in feminism and the privilege of partial perspective. *Feminist Studies, 14,* 575–599.

Harding, S. (2003). A world of sciences. In S. Harding & R. Figueroa (Eds.), *Science and other cultures: Issues in philosophy of science and technology.* New York, NY: Routledge.

Harding, S. (2004). A socially relevant philosophy of science? Resources from standpoint theory's controversiality. *Hypatia, 19*(1), 25–47.

Harding, S. (2006). *Animate earth: Science, intuition and Gaia.* White River Junction, VT: Chelsea Green Publishing.

Harding, S. (2008). *Sciences from below: Feminisms, postcolonialities, and modernities.* Raleigh, NC: Duke University Press.

Hare-Mustin, R. (1994). Discourses in the mirrored room: A postmodern analysis of therapy. *Family Process, 33,* 19–35.

Hartley, G. (2010). The curandera of conquest: Gloria Anzaldúa's decolonial remedy. *Aztlan, 35*(1), 135–161.

Helms, J. E., Nicholas, G., & Green, C. E. (2010). Racism and ethnoviolence as trauma: Enhancing professional training. *Traumatology, 16*(4), 53–62. doi: 10.1177/1534765610389595

Henningsen, P., & Kirmayer, L. J. (2000). Mind beyond the net: Implications of cognitive neuroscience for cultural psychiatry. *Transcultural Psychiatry, 37* (4), 467–494.

Herman, J. L. (1992). *Trauma and recovery.* New York, NY: BasicBooks.

Hernández, P. (2002a). Trauma in war and political persecution: Expanding the concept. *American Journal of Orthopsychiatry, 72*(1), 16–25.

Hernández, P. (2002b). Resilience in families and communities: Latin American contributions from the psychology of liberation. *The Family Journal, 10*(3), 334–343.

Hernández, P. (2004). The cultural context model in supervision: An illustration. *Journal of Feminist Family Therapy, 15*(4), 1–18.

Hernández, P., & McDowell, T. (2010). Intersectionality, power and relational safety: Key concepts in clinical supervision. *Training and Education in Professional Psychology, 4*(1), 29–35. doi: 10.103/a0017064

Hernández-Wolfe, P. (2011). Decolonization and "mental" health: A Mestiza's journey in the borderlands. *Women and Psychology, 34*(3), 293–306.

Hernández, P., Almeida, R. V., & Dolan-Del Vecchio, K. (2005). Critical consciousness, accountability, and empowerment: Key processes for helping families heal. *Family Process, 44*(1), 105–119.

Hernández-Wolfe, P., & McDowell, T. (2012). Speaking of privilege: Family therapy educators' journeys toward awareness and compassionate action. *Family Process, 51*(2), 163–178.

Hernández, P., & Rankin, P. (2008). Relational safety in supervision. *Journal of Marital and Family Therapy, 34*(2), 58–74.

Hochschild, A., & Machung, A. (1989). *The second shift*. New York, NY: Penguin Books.

Hofbauer, A. (2003). O conceito de "raça" e o ideário do "branqueamento"no século XIX–Bases ideológicas do racismo brasileiro. *Teoria de pesquisa*. São Carlos-SP: UFSCar.

Hollander, N. C. (1997). *Love in a time of hate*. New Brunswick, NJ: Rutgers University Press.

hooks, b. (1992). *Black looks: Race and representation*. Boston, MA: South End.

Hopkins, F. (1993). Stress and coping: The influence of racism on the cognitive appraisal processing of African Americans. *Issues in Mental Health Nursing, 14*(4), 399–409.

Humanas. (2011). Nacional de opinión de las mujeres "percepción de las mujeres sobre su situación y condiciones de vida en Chile 2011." Retrieved from http://www.humanas.cl/?page_id=275

Icaza, J. (1999). *Huasipungo*. México: Fondo de Cultura Económica.

Intemann, K. (2010). 25 years of feminist empiricism and standpoint theory: Where are we now? Hypatia, 25(4), 778–796.

International Community for Ecopsychology [website]. (2012) Retrieved from http://www.ecopsychology.org

Jasso-Aguilar, R., Waitzkin, M., & Landwehr, L. (2004). Multinational corporations and health care in the United States and Latin America: Strategies, actions, and effects. *Journal of Health and Social Behavior, 45,* 136–157.

Keating, A. L. (2006). From borderlands and new Mestizas to nepantlas and nepantleras: Anzaldúan theories for social change. *Journal of the Sociology of Self-Knowledge, 4,* 5–16.

Kirmayer, L. J. (2006). Beyond the "new cross-cultural psychiatry": Cultural biology, discursive psychology and the ironies of globalization. *Transcultural Psychiatry, 43*(1), 126–144.

Kirmayer, L. J. (2012a). Culture and context in human rights. In M. Dudley, D. Silove, & F. Gale (Eds.), *Mental health and human rights: Vision, praxis, and courage* (pp. 109–126). Oxford: Oxford University Press.

Kirmayer, L. J. (2012b). Cultural competence and evidence-based practice in mental health: Epistemic communities and the politics of pluralism. *Social Science & Medicine, 75*(2) 249–256.

Kirmayer, L. J., Dandeneau, S., Marshall, E., Phillips, M. K., & Williamson, K. J. (2011). Rethinking resilience from Indigenous perspectives. *La Revue Canadienne de Psychiatrie, 56*(2), 84–91.

Kliman, J. (1994). The interweaving of gender, class and race in family therapy. In M. P. Mirkin (Ed.), *Women in context: Toward a feminist reconstruction of psychotherapy* (pp. 25–47). New York, NY: Guilford Press.

Laird, J. (1989). Women and stories: Restoring women's self constructions. In M. McGoldrick, C. Anderson, & F. Walsh (Eds.), *Women in families* (pp. 427–450). New York, NY: W. W. Norton.

Landrine, H., & Klonoff, E. A. (1996). The schedule of racist events. *Journal of Black Psychology, 22,* 144-168.

Leacock, E. (2008). *Myths of male dominance: Collected articles on women cross-culturally.* Chicago, IL: Haymarket Books.

Liebenberg, L., & Ungar, M. (2009). Introduction: The challenges in researching resilience. In M. Ungar & L. Liebenberg (Eds.), *Researching resilience* (pp. 3–25). Toronto and Buffalo: University of Toronto Press.

Lionnet, F., & Shih, S. (2005). *Minor transnationalism.* Durham, NC: Duke University Press.

Lira, E. (2002). Notas sobre psicología crítica. In I. Piper (Ed.), *Políticas, sujetos y resistencias: Debates y críticas en psicología social* (pp. 255–266). Santiago: ARCIS.

Lomax, A. (1977). Appeal for cultural equity. *Journal of Communication, 27*(2),125–138.

López, M. (1992). Ajuste de cuentas con la psicología social-comunitaria: Balance a diez años. En I. García de Serrano & W. Rosario Collazo (Eds.), *Contribuciones puertorriqueñas a la psicología social-comunitaria* (pp. 107–116). San Juan: Editorial de la Universidad de Puerto Rico.

Loveman, M. (2009). Whiteness in Latin America: Measurement and meaning in national censuses (1850–1950). *Journal de la Société des Américanistes, 95*(2), 1–30.

Loveman, M., & Muniz, J. O. (2007). How Puerto Rico became White: Boundary dynamics and intercensus racial reclassification. *American Sociological Review, 72*(6), 915–939.

Luepnitz, D. A. (1988). *The family interpreted: Feminist theory in clinical practice.* New York, NY: Basic Books.

Lugones, M. (1992). On borderlands/la frontera: An interpretive essay. *Hypatia, 7*(4), 31–37.

Lugones, M. (2003). *Peregrinajes/pilgrimages: Theorizing coalition against multiple oppressions.* New York, NY: Rowman & Littlefield.

Lugones, M. (2005). Radical multiculturalism and women of color feminisms. *Revista Internacional de Filosofía Política, 25*, 61–75.

Lugones, M. (2007). Heterosexualism and the colonial/modern gender system. *Hypatia, 22*(1), 186–209.

Lugones, M. (2010). Toward a decolonial feminism. *Hypatia, 25*(4), 742–749.

Lum, D. (2007). *Culturally competent practice: A framework for understanding diverse groups and justice issues.* Belmont, CA: Brooks/Cole.

Luna, L. E. (1986). *Vegetalismo: Shamanism among the Mestizo population of the Peruvian Amazon.* Stockholm, Sweden: Acta Universitatis Stockholmiensis.

Luthar, S., & Cicchetti, D. (2000). The construct of resilience: Implications for interventions and social policies. *Development and Psychopathology, 12* (4), 857–885. doi: 10.1017/S0954579400004156

Luthar, S., & Zelazo, L. B. (2003). Research on resilience: An integrative review. In S. S. Luthar (Ed.), *Resilience and vulnerability: Adaptation in the context of childhood adversities.* (pp. 510–550). Cambridge, UK: Cambridge University Press.

Mack, J. E. (1995). The politics of species arrogance. In T. Roszak, M. E. Gomes, & A. D. Kanner (Eds.), *Ecopsychology: Restoring the earth, healing the mind* (pp. 279–287). San Francisco, CA: Sierra Club Books.

Macy, J. (1983). *Despair and personal power in the nuclear age.* Philadelphia, PA: New Society Publications.

Maher, M. (Director and Producer). (2011, December 1). *Unlawful justice: The story of Antjuanece Brown and Jolene Jenkins* [video documentary]. Presented at Growing Up Policed: Surveilling Racialized Sexualities Videoconference, with City University of New York, University of Oregon, and Lewis & Clark College.

Maldonado-Torres, N. (2005). Liberation theology and the search for the lost paradigm: From radical orthodoxy to radical diversality. In Ivan Petrella (Ed.), *Latin American liberation theology: The next generation* (pp. 39–61). Maryknoll, NY: Orbis Books.

Mann, C. (2005). *1491: New revelations of the Americas before Columbus.* New York, NY: Vintage Books.

Marcos, S. & Le Bot, Y. (1997). *El sueno zapatista.* QuedeLibros.com

Martín-Alcoff, L., Hames-García, M., Mohanty, S., & Moya, P. (2006). *Identity politics reconsidered.* New York, NY: Palgrave Macmillan.

Martín-Baró, I. (1982). A social psychologist faces the civil war in El Salvador. *Revista Latinoamericana de Psicología, 2*(1), 90–111.

Martín-Baró, I. (1984). Guerra y salud mental. *Estudios Centroamericanos, 39*, 503–514.

Martín-Baró, I. (1986). Hacia una psicología social de la liberación. *Boletín de Psicología de El Salvador, 5*(22), 219–231.

Martín-Baró, I. (1988). Los grupos con historia: Un modelo psicosocial. *Boletín de la Asociación Venezolana de Psicología Social (AVEPSO), 11*(1), 3–18.

Martín-Baró, I. (1989). Political violence and war as causes of psychosocial trauma in El Salvador. *International Journal of Mental Health, 18*(1), 3–20.

Martín-Baró, I. (1990). *Psicología social de la guerra: Trauma y terapia.* San Salvador, El Salvador: UCA Editores.

Martín-Baró, I. (1994). *Writings for a liberation psychology.* Cambridge, MA: Harvard University Press.

Martín-Baró, I. (1995). Procesos psíquicos y poder. In O. D'Adamo, B. V. García, & M. Montero, *Psicología de la acción política* (pp. 205–233). Buenos Aires, Argentina: Paidós.

Masson, J. M. (2010). *The dog who couldn't stop loving: How dogs have captured our hearts for thousands of years.* New York, NY: HarperCollins.

Maté, G. (2003). *When the body says no: Exploring the stress-disease connection.* Hoboken, New Jersey: John Wiley & Sons.

Maté, G. (2010). *In the realm of hungry ghosts.* Berkeley, CA: North Atlantic Books.

Masten, A. S. (1994). Resilience in individual development: Successful adaptation despite risk and adversity. In M. Wang & E. Gordon (Eds.), *Educational resilience in inner-city America: Challenges and prospects* (pp. 3–25). Hillsdale, NJ: Erlbaum.

Masten, A. S. (2001). Ordinary magic: Resilience processes in development. *American Psychologist, 56* (3), 227–238. doi: 10.1037/0003-066X.56.3.227

McCardle, P., McCune, S., Netting, F. E., Berger, A., & Maholmes, V. (2011). Therapeutic human-animal interaction: An overview. In P. McCardle, S. McCune, J. A. Griffin, L. Esposito, & L. S. Freund. (Eds.), *Animals in our lives: Human–animal interaction in family, community, and therapeutic settings* (pp. 107–115). Baltimore, MD: Paul H. Brooke.

McEwen, B. (2000). The neurobiology of stress: From serendipity to clinical relevance. *Brain Research, 886*, 172–189.

McGoldrick, M., Anderson, C., & Walsh, C. (1991). *Women in families: A framework for family therapy.* New York, NY: W. W. Norton.

McGoldrick, M., Gerson, R., & Petry, S. S. (2008). *Genograms: Assessment and intervention* (3rd ed.). New York, NY: W. W. Norton.

McNeill, B., & Cervantes, J. (2008). *Latina/o healing practices: Mestizo and indigenous perspectives.* New York, NY: Routledge/Taylor & Francis Group.

McNeill, B., Esquivel, E., Carrasco, A., & Mendoza, R. (2008). Santeria and the healing process in Cuba and United States. In B. W. McNeill & J. Cervantes (Eds.), *Latina/o healing practices: Mestizo and indigenous perspectives* (pp. 63–80). New York, NY: Routledge/Taylor & Francis Group.

Mesa, G., Sanchez, L. F., Ruiz, A. F., & Cabra, S. A. (2011). Autonomia indígena y derechos colectivos: El caso de la prestación del servicio de educación a los pueblos indígenas. In G. Mesa. (Ed.), *Elementos para una teoría de la justicia ambiental y el estado ambiental de derecho* (pp. 572–585). Bogotá, Colombia: Universidad Nacional.

Mignolo, W. (2000a). Coloniality at large: Time and the colonial difference. In *Time in the making and possible futures*, E. Rodriquez Larreta (Ed.), Rio de Janeiro: UNESCO-ISSC-EDUCAM.

Mignolo, W. (2000b). *Local histories/global designs: Coloniality, subaltern knowledges, and border thinking.* Princeton, NJ: Princeton University Press.

Mignolo, W. (2000c). The many faces of cosmo-polis: Border thinking and critical cosmopolitanism. *Public Culture, 12*(3), 721–748.

Mignolo, W. (2005). *The idea of Latin America.* New York, NY: Blackwell.

Mignolo, W. (2006). Introduction. In Walsh, C., Mignolo, W., & Linera, A. G., (Eds.), *Interculturalidad, descolonización del estado y conocimiento.* Buenos Aires, Argentina: Ediciones del Signo.

Mignolo, W. (2007). The decolonial option and the meaning of identity. *Anales Nueva Epoca* (Instituto Iberoamericano Universidad de Goteborg), *9/10*, 43–72.

Mignolo, W. (2009a). Epistemic disobedience, independent thought and de-colonial freedom. *Theory, Culture & Society, 26*(7–8), 1–23.

Mignolo, W. (2009b). The communal and the decolonial. *Turbulence, 5*. Retrieved from http://turbulence.org.uk/turbulence-5/decolonial/

Mignolo, W. (2010, April). *Globalization and the geopolitics of knowing: A decolonial view of the Humanitie*. Hilldale Lectures in the Arts and Humanities, the University of Wisconsin at Madison.

Mignolo, W. (2011). Geopolitics of sensing and knowing: On (de)coloniality, border thinking and epistemic disobedience. *Postcolonial Studies, 14*(3), 273–285.

Mignolo, W., & Tlostanova, M. (2006). Theorizing from the border: Shifting to the geo/body-politics of knowledge. *European Journal of Social Theory, 9*(2), 205–221.

Minuchin, S., & Fishman, H. C. (1981). *Family therapy techniques*. Boston, MA: Harvard University Press.

Miranda, D. (2010). Extermination of the Joyas: Gendercide in Spanish California. *Journal of Lesbian and Gay Studies, 16*(1–2), 253–284.

Mirkin, M. P. (1994). Introduction. In M. P. Mirkin (Ed.), *Women in context: Toward a feminist reconstruction of psychotherapy* (pp. 1–25). New York, NY: Guilford Press.

Mohanty, C. (2003). *Feminism without borders*. Durham, NC, and London, UK: Duke University Press.

Monk, G., Winslade, J., & Sinclair, S. (2008). *New horizons in multicultural counseling*. Thousand Oaks, CA: Sage.

Montero, M. (1980). La psicología social y el desarrollo de comunidades en América Latina. *Revista Latinoamericana de Psicología, 12*(1), 159–170.

Montero, M. (1982). La psicología comunitaria: Orígenes, principios y fundamentos teóricos. *Boletín de la Asociación Venezolana de Psicología Social (AVEPSO), 5*(1), 15–22.

Montero, M. (1992). Psicología de la liberación. Propuesta para una teoría sociopsicológica. En U. H. Riquelme (Ed.), *Otras realidades, otras vías de acceso: Psicología y psiquiatría transcultural en América Latina* (pp. 133–150). Caracas: Ed. Nueva Sociedad.

Montero, M. (1999). De la realidad, la verdad y otras ilusiones concretas: Para una epistemología de la psicología social comunitaria. *Psykhe, 8*(1), 9–18.

Montero, M. (2004). Relaciones entre psicología social comunitaria, psicología crítica y psicología de la liberación: Una respuesta Latinoamericana. *Psykhe, 13*(2), 17–28.

Montero, M., & Serrano-García, I. (2011). *Historia de la psicología comunitaria en América Latina*. Barcelona, Spain: Paidós.

Moraga, C. (2011). *A Xicana codex of changing consciousness*. Durham, NC: Duke University Press.

Nensthiel, C. (2012). *Encuentros de voces: Dispositivos de intervención que responden al sufrimiento de un sujeto colectivo* (Unpublished master's thesis). Universidad Javeriana, Bogotá, Colombia.

Nesmith, A. A., Burton, D. L., & Cosgrove, T. J. (1999). Gay, lesbian, and bisexual youth and youth adults: Social support in their own words. *Journal of Homosexuality, 37*(1), 95–108.

Park, Y. and Kemp, S.P. (2006). "Little Alien Colonies": Representations of Immigrants and Their Neighborhoods in Social Work Discourse, 1875-1924. *Social Service Review*. 80 (4), 705-734.

Parker, L. (2003). Bringing power from the margins to the center. In L. B. Silverstein and T. J. Goodrich (Eds.), *Feminist family therapy: Empowerment in social context* (pp. 225–238). Washington, DC: American Psychological Association.

Parker, L. (2009). Disrupting power and privilege in couples' therapy. *Clinical Social Work Journal, 37*(3), 248–255.

Pedersen, D., Tremblay, J., Errazuriz, C., & Gamarra, J. (2008). The sequelae of political violence: Assessing trauma, suffering and dislocation in the Peruvian highlands. *Social Science & Medicine , 67*(2), 205–217.

Pérez, E. (1999). *The decolonial imaginary: Writing Chicanas into history*. Bloomberg, IN: Indiana University Press.

Pérez, E. (2003). Borderland queers: The challenges of excavating the invisible and unheard. *Frontiers: A Journal of Women's Studies, 24*(2/3), 122–131.

Pew Institute. (2009). *A rising share: Hispanics and federal crime*. Retrieved from http:// ipsnews.net/news.asp?idnews=104877

Prakash, G. (1999). *Another reason: Science and the imagination of modern India*. Princeton, NJ: Princeton University Press.

Prilleltensky, I., & Nelson, G. (2002). *Doing psychology critically*. New York: Palgrave Mac-Millan.

Prilleltensky, I., & Prilleltensky, O. (2006). *Promoting well-being: Linking personal, organizational and community change*. Hoboken, NJ: John Wiley.

Quijano, A. (2000a). Colonialidad del poder y clasificación social. *Journal of World-Systems Research, XI*(2), 342–386.

Quijano, A. (2000b). Coloniality of power, Eurocentrism, and Latin America. *Nepantla, 1*(3), 533–580.

Reichel-Dolmatoff, G. (1997). *Rainforest shamans: Essays on the Tukano Indians of the Northwest Amazon*. London, UK: Themis Books.

Rober, P., & Seltzer, M. (2010). Avoiding the colonizing positions in the therapy room: Some ideas about the challenges of dealing with the dialectic of misery and resources in families. *Family Process, 49*(1), 123–137. doi: 10.1111/j.1545-5300.2010.01312.x

Roberto-Forman, L. (2008). Transgenerational couple therapy. In A. S. Gurman & N. S. Jacobson (Eds.), *Clinical handbook of couple therapy* (pp. 196–230). New York, NY: Guilford Press.

Rodriguez, I. (2007). Creolization, hybridity, pluralism: Historical articulations of race and ethnicity. In A. Paul (Ed.), *Caribbean culture: Soundings on Kamau Brathwaite* (pp. 235–245). Kingston, Jamaica: University of the West Indies Press.

Rosaldo, R. (2008). *Anthropology of globalization*. New York, NY: Wiley-Blackwell.

Roszak, T. (1995). Where Psyche meets Gaia. In T. Roszak, M. E. Gomes, & A. D. Kanner (Eds.), *Ecopsychology: Restoring the earth, healing the mind* (pp. 263–278). San Francisco, CA: Sierra Club Books.

Rotker, S. (1999). *Cautivas: Olvidos y memoria en al Argentina*. Buenos Aires, Argentina: Editora Espasa Calpe.

Roy, A. (2004). *An ordinary person's guide to empire*. Minneapolis, MN: Consortium Publishers.

Russell, S. T. (2005). Beyond risk: Resilience in the lives of sexual minority youth. *Journal of Gay & Lesbian Issues in Education, 2*(3), 5–18.

Ryu, E. (2010). *Sponsoring change in self and others: Female sponsors in the cultural context model* (Unpublished doctoral dissertation). Drexel University, Philadelphia, PA.

Sabin, M., Cardozo, B. L., Nackerud, L., Kaiser, R., & Varese, L. (2003). Factors associated with poor mental health among Guatemalan refugees living in Mexico 20 years after civil conflict. *Journal of the American Medical Association, 290*(5), 635–642.

Said, E. (1978). *Orientalism*. New York, NY: Vintage Books.

Sandoval, C. (2001). *Methodology of the oppressed*. Minneapolis, MN: University of Minnesota Press.

Santos, B. S. (2004a). *The world's social forum user's manual*. Madison, WI: University of Wisconsin.

Santos, B. S. (2004b). The future of the world social forum. *La Rivista del Manifesto, 47*. Retrieved from http://www.larivistadelmanifesto.it/originale/47A20040203.html

Santos, B. S. (2006). *The rise of the of the global left*. United Kingdom: Zed Books.

Santos, B. S. (2009). *Una Epistemología del Sur: La reinvención del conocimiento y la emancipación social*. Buenos Aires, Argentina: Siglo XXI Editores.

Santos, B. S. (2010). *Refundación del estado en América Latina: Perspectivas desde una epistemología del sur*. México: Siglo XXI Editores.

Schaefer, T. (2008). *Encyclopedia of race, ethnicity, and society*. Thousand Oaks, CA: Sage.

Schwarz, Á. C. (2012). *Decolonization models for America's last colony: Puerto Rico*. Syracuse, NY: Syracuse University Press.

Shanon, B. (2002). *The antipodes of the mind: Charting the phenomenology of the ayahuasca experience*. Oxford: Oxford University Press.

Shepard, B., O'Neill, L., & Guenette, F. (2006). Counseling with First Nations women: Considerations of oppression and renewal. *International Journal for the Advancement of Counselling, 28*(3), 227–240. doi: 10.1007/s10447-005-9008-8

Shepard, M., and Pence, E. (1999). *Coordinating commnunity response to domestic violence: Lessons from Duluth and beyond. Sage series on violence against women.* Thousand Oaks, CA: Sage.

Siegel, D. J. (1999). *The developing mind: Toward a neurobiology of interpersonal experience.* New York, NY: Guilford Press.

Siegel, D. J. (2007a). Mindfulness training and neural integration: Differentiation of distinct streams of awareness and the cultivation of well-being. *Social, Cognitive and Affective Neuroscience, 2*(4), 259–263.

Siegel, D. J. (2007b). *The mindful brain: Reflection and attunement in the cultivation of well-being.* New York, NY: W. W. Norton.

Siegel, D. J., & Hartzell, M. (2003). *Parenting from the inside out: How a deeper self-understanding can help you raise children who thrive.* New York, NY: J. P. Tarcher/Putnam.

Smith, L. T. (1999). *Decolonizing methodologies: Research and indigenous peoples.* London, UK: Zed.

Stephen, L., & Tula, M. T. (1994). *Hear my testimony: Maria Teresa Tula, human rights activist of El Salvador.* Boston, MA: South End Press.

Stubbs, J., & Reyes, H. N. (2006). *Más allá de los promedios: Afrodescendientes en América Latina: Resultados de la Prueba Piloto de Captación en la Argentina.* Buenos Aires, Argentina: Universidad Nacional de Tres de Febrero.

Suarez-Ojeda, E. N. (2001). Una concepción Latinoamericana: La resiliencia comunitaria. In M. A. de Paladini, A. Melillo, & E. N. Suarez Ojeda (Eds.), *Resiliencia: Descubriendo las propias fortalezas* (pp. 67–82). Barcelona, Spain: Paidós.

Sugawara, A., Masud, M. M., Yokoyama, A., Mizutani, W., Watanuki, S., Yanai, K., Itoh, M., & Tashiro, M. (2012). Effects of presence of a familiar pet dog on regional cerebral activity in healthy volunteers: A positron emission tomography study. *Anthrozoös, 25*(1), 25–34. doi: 10.2752/175303712X13240472427311

Summerfield, D. (1995). Addressing human response to war and atrocity: Major challenges in research and practice and the limitations of Western psychiatric models. In R. J. Kleber, C. Figley, & B. Gersons, (Eds.), *Beyond trauma: Cultural and societal dynamics*, (pp. 17–29). New York, NY: Plenum Press.

Summerfield, D. (2004). Cross-cultural perspectives on the medicalization of human suffering. In G. Rosen (Ed.), *Posttraumatic stress disorder: Issues and controversies* (pp. 233–245). Southern Gate, Chichester, UK: John Wiley.

Tamasese, K., Peteru, C., Waldegrave, C., & Bush, A. (2005). Ole Taeao Afua, the new morning: A qualitative investigation into Samoan perspectives on mental health and culturally appropriate services. *Australian and New Zealand Journal of Psychiatry, 39*(4), 300–309.

Tamasese, K., & Waldegrave, C. (2003). Cultural and gender accountability in the Just Therapy approach. In C. Waldegrave, K. Tamasese, F. Tuhaka, & W. Campbell (Eds.), *Just therapy—A journey: A collection of papers from the Just Therapy team* (pp. 81–96). Adelaide, Australia: Dulwich Centre Publications.

Tamasese, K., & Waldegrave, C. (2008). *Culture and gender accountability in the Just Therapy approach.* Paper presented at the Annual Liberation Based Therapy Conference, Johns Hopkins University, Baltimore, MD.

Tervalon, M., & Murray-Garcia, J. (1998). Cultural humility versus cultural competence: A critical distinction in defining physician training outcomes in multicultural education. *Journal of Health Care for the Poor and Underserved, 9*(2), 117–125.

Todorov, T. (1987). *The conquest of America: The question of the other.* New York, NY: Harper Torchbooks.

Tupper, K. (2009). Ayahuasca healing beyond the Amazon: The globalization of a traditional indigenous entheogenic practice. *Global Networks, 9*(1),117–136.

U.S. Department of Justice. (2000). *A resource guide on racial profiling collection data systems: Promising practices and lessons learned.* Washington, DC: U.S. Department of Justice.

Ungar, M. (2008). Resilience across cultures, *British Journal of Social Work, 38*(2), 218–235.

Ungar, M., Lee, A. W., Callaghan, T., & Boothroyd, R. A. (2005). An international collaboration to study resilience in adolescents across cultures. *Journal of Social Work Research and Evaluation, 6*(1), 5–23.

United Nations Development Programme. (2008). *Assessment of development results: Evaluation of UNDP contributions: Ecuador.* United States: Author.

University of Minnesota. (2012). *Driven to discover.* Retrieved from http://voices.cla.umn.edu/artistpages/anzaldua.php

Uribe, C. A. (2008). El yajé, el purgatorio y la farándula. *Antípoda, 6,* 113–131.

Utsey, S. O., Chae, M. H., Brown, C. F., & Kelly, D. (2002). Effect of ethnic group membership on ethnic identity, race-related stress, and quality of life. *Cultural Diversity and Ethnic Minority Psychology, 8,* 366–377.

Utsey, S. O., Ponterotto, J. G., Reynolds, A. L., & Cancelli, A. A. (2000). Racial discrimination, coping, life satisfaction, and self-esteem among African Americans. *Journal of Counseling and Development, 78,* 72–80.

Van der Kolk, B. A. (1984). *Post-traumatic stress disorder: Psychological and biological sequelae.* Washington DC: American Psychiatric Press.

Varner, J. G., & Johnson, J. J. (1983). *Dogs of the conquest.* Norman, OK: University of Oklahoma Press.

Wade, P. (2008). Race in Latin America. In D. Poole (Ed.), *Companion to Latin American anthropology* (pp. 177–192). New York, NY: Blackwell.

Wade, P. (2010). *Race and ethnicity in Latin America* (2nd ed.) London, UK: Pluto Press.

Waldegrave, C. (2003). Just Therapy. In C. Waldegrave, K. Tamasese, F. Tuhaka, & W. Campbell (Eds.), *Just Therapy—a journey: A collection of papers from the Just Therapy team* (pp. 3–64). Adelaide, Australia: Dulwich Centre Publications.

Waldegrave, C. (2009). Cultural, gender and socio-economic contexts in therapeutic and social policy work. *Family Process, 48*(1), 85–101.

Waldegrave, C., King, P., Walker, T., & Fizgerlad, E. (2006). *Maori housing experiences: Emerging trends and issues.* New Zealand: Centre for Housing Research.

Waldegrave, C., & Stephens, R. (2000). Poverty: The litmus test of social and economic policy failure. In *Conference Proceedings of the Second Bienniel Aotearoa New Zealand International Development Studies Network (DEVNET) Conference 17–19 November 2000 at Victoria University of Wellington,* DEVNET, Wellington. Retrieved from www.devnet.org.nz/conf/Papers/waldegrave.pdf

Waldegrave, C., Stephens, R., & King, P. (2003). Assessing the progress of poverty reduction. *Social Policy Journal of New Zealand, 20,* 197–222.

Waldegrave, C., & Tamasese, K. (1994). Some central ideas in the Just Therapy approach. *The Family Journal: Counseling and Therapy for Couples and Families, 2*(2), 94–103.

Waldegrave, C., Tamasese, K., Tuhaha, F., and Campbell, W. (Eds.). (2003). *Just Therapy—a journey: A collection of papers from the Just Therapy team.* Adelaide, Australia: Dulwich Centre Publications.

Walker, L. (2005). Exporting a problem: Gang members deported from U.S. take deadly culture to their home countries. *San Diego Union Tribune.* Retrieved from http://www.utsandiego.com/uniontrib/20050116/news_lz1n16export.html

Waller, I. (1996). Victims of crime: Justice, support and public safety. In Y. Danieli, N. S. Rodley, & L. Weisaeth (Eds.), *International responses to traumatic stress* (pp. 81–129). New York, NY: Baywood Publishing.

Walsh, F. (2002). *Normal family processes: Growing diversity and complexity* (3rd ed.). New York, NY; London, UK: Guilford Press.

Walsh, F. (2006). *Strengthening family resilience* (2nd ed.). New York, NY: Guilford Press.

Walsh, F. (2009a). Human-animal bonds I: The relational significance of companion animals. *Family Process, 48*(4), 462–480.

Walsh, F. (2009b). Human-animal bonds II: The role of pets in family systems and family therapy. *Family Process*, *48*(4), 481–499.

Weingarten, K. (1991). The discourses of intimacy: Adding a social constructionist and feminist view. *Family Process, 30*, 285–305.

Weingarten, K. (1995). Radical listening: Challenging cultural beliefs for and about mothers. In K. Weingarten (Ed.), *Cultural resistance: Challenging beliefs about women, men and therapy* (pp. 7–22). Binghamton, NY: Haworth Press.

Weingarten, K. (2003). *Common shock: Witnessing violence every day*. New York, NY: Penguin Group.

Wexler, L., DiFulvio, G. T., & Burke, T. (2009). Resilience and marginalized youth: Making a case for personal and collective meaning-making as part of resilience research in public health. *Social Science & Medicine, 69*(4), 565–570.

Wiechelt, S., Gryczynski, J., Johnson, J., & Caldwell, D. (2012). Historical trauma among urban American Indians: Impact on substance abuse and family cohesion. *Journal of Loss and Trauma, 17*(4), 319–336. doi: 10.1080/15325024.2011.616837

Wiesner-Hanks, M. E. (2000). *Christianity and sexuality in the early modern world*. New York, NY: Routledge.

Winkler, D., & Cueto, S. (2004). *Etnicidad, raza, género y educación en América Latina*. Santiago de Chile: PREAL.

Wylie, A. (2001). Doing social science as a feminist: The engendering of archaeology. In A. Creager, E. Lunbeck, & L. Schiebinger (Eds.), *Feminism in twentieth century science, technology, and medicine* (pp. 23–45). Chicago, IL: University of Chicago Press.

Wylie, A. (2003). Why standpoint matters. In R. Figueroa & S. Harding (Eds.), *Science and other cultures: Issues in philosophies of science and technology* (pp. 339–351). New York, NY: Routledge.

Yehuda, R. (2002). Post-traumatic stress disorder. *New England Journal of Medicine, 346*(2), 108–114.

Yehuda, R., & Bierer, L. M. (2008). Transgenerational transmission of cortisol and PTSD risk. *Progress in Brain Research, 167*, 121–135.

Yehuda, R., & Flory, J. D. (2007). Differentiating biological correlates of risk, PTSD, and resilience following trauma exposure. *Journal of Traumatic Stress, 20*(4), 435–447.

Yehuda, R., & LeDoux, J. (2007). Response variation following trauma: A translational neuroscience approach to understanding PTSD. *Neuron, 56*(1), 19–32.

Yehuda R, Teicher, M. H., Seckl, J. R., Grossman, R. A., Morris, A., & Bierer, L. M. (2007). Parental PTSD as a vulnerability factor for low cortisol trait in offspring of holocaust survivors. *Archives of General Psychiatry, 64*(9), 1040–1048.

Yehuda, R., Schmeidler, J., Elkin, A., Wilson, G. S., Siever, L., Binder-Brynes, K., Wainberg, M., & Aferiot, D. (1998). Phenomenology and psychobiology of the intergenerational response to trauma. In Y. Danieli (Ed.), *International handbook of multigenerational legacies of trauma. The Plenum series on stress and coping* (pp. 639–655). New York, NY: Plenum Press.

Yellowbird, M. J. (2001). Critical values and First Nations peoples. In R. Fong & S. Furuto (Eds.), *Culturally competent practice: Skills, interventions, and evaluations* (pp. 61–74). Boston, MA: Allyn & Bacon.

Zavaleta, A., Salinas, A., Jr., & Sams, J. (2009). *Curandero conversations: El niño fidencio, shamanism and healing traditions of the borderlands*. Bloomington, IN: Author House.

Index

About the Author

Pilar Hernández-Wolfe, PhD, is an educator, researcher, therapist, speaker, author, consultant, and community organizer. She is associate professor and director of the Marriage, Couple, and Family Therapy program at Lewis & Clark College. She is past president of the Maryland Association for Counseling and Development (MACD) and board member of the American Family Therapy Academy (AFTA). She is a licensed marriage and family therapist and an American Association for Marriage and Family Therapy (AAMFT) approved supervisor. She has authored or coauthored over forty peer-reviewed article, and book chapters in English and Spanish.

Pilar earned her bachelor's degree at the Universidad de Los Andes in Bogotá, Colombia, and her doctorate in Counseling Psychology at the University of Massachusetts at Amherst. She is a faculty member at the Institute for Family Services, where she provides training and supervision, and directs research projects on liberation-based healing. She is also a guest faculty member at the Centro de Terapia Familiar y de Pareja in Puebla, México, and at the Universidad Javeriana, Cali, and Universidad Nacional, Bogotá, in Colombia. Her theoretical work examines applications of contextually responsive models to clinical practice and clinical supervision. Her research areas include domestic violence, resilience, vicarious resilience, traumatic stress, and human rights. She pioneered the concept of vicarious resilience in the context of torture-survivor treatment with Drs. David Gangsei and David Engstrom.